STAFFORDSHIRE
STONE
RUGELEY
LICHFIELD
WARWICKSHIRE
SHROPSHIRE
NUNEATON
← HAWKESBURY JUNC.
COVENTRY
RUGBY
← BRAUNSTON JUNC.
NAPTON JUNC. →
BANBURY
OXFORDSHIRE
OXFORD
LONDON
BERKSHIRE
HENLEY
PANGBOURNE
HAMPTON C.

MAID MARYSUE

ENGLISH CHANNEL

AND A RIGHT GOOD CREW

BOOKS BY EMILY KIMBROUGH

AND A RIGHT
GOOD CREW

BY EMILY KIMBROUGH

Drawings by Mircea Vasiliu

Harper & Brothers Publishers, New York

PREFACE

Not long ago I overheard a friend say, "I love to hear about a trip people are planning to take, but I hope they will not tell me about it when they come home. I like beginnings, not endings."

I consider this a disconcerting but understandable point of view. It is one, however, I do not share. I want to know how things turn out; books, plays or expeditions.

I cannot speak for the novelist or the playwright, but as a traveler on a small scale—I have never planted a flag on peak or pole, nor explored the upper reaches of anything—I consider the accomplishment of a trip far easier to recite than its beginning, though even then I am none too stable in specific recapitulation. If anyone pointing a figurative finger at me, and I have had this happen, asks, "What do you consider the best novel you have read in the last ten years?" I cannot remember having read anything since the *Jungle Books* and *The Wind in the Willows*. Let someone impale me with the question of what islands in Greece I visited and my memory is sponged clean of names. They will in time come through to the surface, but not by means of a calculated harking back. A haphazard detail first, then the name will attach itself. A courtyard dappled in sunlight, a curving staircase at the end, its banister dripping yellow flowers, and ragged, beautiful children playing on its steps; that was Rhodes. I shared a bath-house with a large spider; that was on the beach at Crete.

Such trivia are for me identification marks of places I have visited; but the marks that identify the beginning of a trip are not so easily recalled. They require deeper excavation. At what moment does anyone change "Someday I want to go to Spain" to "I'm going to Spain this spring"? For that matter, what prompted the incipient traveler to choose Spain? Perhaps that moment of choice is the real beginning of a trip. Therefore, how far back must one go to make a running start toward the recital of the trip itself?

There may be something of the ancient mariner in me that urges my telling of a trip after it is over; but I prefer to believe the motivation for setting this one down is the hope that, reading it, one Mary Smith or whatever her name and wherever she lives will say to her husband, "John, why don't we do this?" Perhaps they will, and if they do they will know, not adventure, but an idyll that for the rest of their lives will remain an image set apart from time in a still pond of tranquillity.

x

AND A RIGHT GOOD CREW

CHAPTER ONE

I CANNOT empty the garbage," Arthur Kober said, "because I had an unhappy childhood, poor and underprivileged. If I am reminded of it I might have to send for my analyst." He looked speculatively at Sophy on the other side of the fireplace, "Now you," he began, "come from—" Sophy interrupted. "Skip it," she told him wearily. "It's never been by way of a psychoanalyst before, but somehow or other I'm always the one who carries the slops." Arthur settled back happily. "You see," he told the group, "Sophy is well adjusted."

There were five of us that February evening in Sophy's apartment. We had gathered to learn from her our route on the English canals and talk with one another about what we would take with us and where we would meet. Until the moment of Arthur's announced abnegation it had not occurred to any of us we must include in our discussion an allotment of offices, but Howard Lindsay was quick to follow the new channel.

"I will be the banker," he proposed. He admitted afterward his nomination was prompted by an apprehension that Sophy might waive Arthur's choice and the post of garbage collector still be vacant. Dorothy, who was sitting beside Arthur on a couch by the fire, leaned forward and around him to look with astonishment at her husband. "Why, Howard," she said, "you've never been able to understand English money." Howard's armchair became a chairman's seat as we turned inquiringly toward this self-nominee. He regarded his wife with somber reproach.

"I know that," he told her, and addressing himself to the group added, "this is an excellent way for me to learn."

I dare say it occurred to the others, as the idea crossed my mind, this method of acquiring knowledge might be of some cost to the depositors, but Howard developed his candidacy. "I have a high regard for money," he assured us, "and concern about the way it is spent. I am not parsimonious, I tip generously, but not ostentatiously. I like to live as comfortably as possible and eat well, therefore I would not be grudging about paying for this, and," he concluded with a deprecatory shake of his head at Dorothy, "whatever my shortcomings or my short changes may be they will not be intentional. I am fundamentally a reasonably honest man."

Arthur considered this, he said, one of the best campaign speeches he had ever heard. Howard was established as Banker Lindsay.

Sophy told the others and me I would be the cook, explaining, without mention of any culinary talent, that I had done the cooking when we had cruised on the Thames and, therefore, was accustomed to working in a small space. Arthur interrupted with a protest that he did not wish to be considered averse to work; only he must confine himself to gentlemanly tasks such as lighting cigarettes or serving drinks, adding generously that Dorothy could help him.

Sophy brought maps, spread them on the floor at our feet, squatted beside them and traced for everyone but me the meandering course we would take.

Pointing to places on a map is of no benefit to me. Confronted by a diagram of, say, France, I do not know in which part of it to start looking for Paris, and when, after an over-all roaming, I do identify it, because the name is printed in larger type than is used for lesser villes, I recognize only that the spot on the diagram says, "Paris."

I had not proposed England in the beginning, nor canals. My proposition simply had been a boat of our own. As the old song says, "Not like a hallroom nor big as a ballroom," I had suggested neither a canoe nor a yacht but a comfortable in-between where we could eat and sleep. As to where the boat should travel I preferred, I said, something with banks on either side that not only were visible but could be reached in emergency within my capacity of fifty swimming strokes. On the other hand fiords though narrow had for me an ominous suggestion of cold water, should I have to feel it, and steep banks. I am a timorous explorer. I had presented my nebulous ideas to Sophy, who is in every sense of the word a mapper. She can plan as well as read.

I had a poodle once who loved dog shows. I had only to ask, "Do you want to go to a dog show?" and within five minutes he had gripped in his teeth and then laid at my feet his show leash, brush, comb, feeding pan, and even dragged out the carrier in which he traveled. Give Sophy

the suggestion "Do you want to go on a trip?" and with some difference she is vividly reminiscent to me of Champion Kennelquest Paul of Cartlane, and I am ankle deep in guidebooks and travel literature.

Eliminating oceans and fiords Sophy had suggested a river. I was amenable to this but outlawed the Nile and the Amazon, too far off, too expensive to reach; I would prefer a homier stream. She tried for the Rhine and the Seine, but reported either of these courses required considerable knowledge of navigation if they were to be sailed by amateurs, or a sizable professional crew and a boat to match. Either of these requirements we pronounced with rueful accord was beyond our personal or financial capacity. We allowed the rivers to shrink down

to canals. Not Holland, because we had each of us traveled there on land and by boat—my water passage mostly on ferries—and this time we wanted an unfamiliar landscape. There are canals in France we knew vaguely and the next time I am in that country I will find out about them; but I defy anyone to learn from correspondence or travel bureaus how one can, as we say in Indiana, "get to go" on them.

The British Travel Association is not reticent about the canals of England and Wales. One telephone call to James Turbayne, the head of that organization in New York, had set off a chain reaction of letters, literature and maps from which I retreated in dismay, but Sophy embraced. Before this wash of literature had risen higher than her instep when Sophy spread it around her, she had received in the mail corroboration of what it promised. A friend sent her an article by Dal Stivens from the July, 1956, number of *House and Garden*. Its title is "England by U-Drive Canal Boat" and its content a chronicle of a trip by the author. The article included an open sesame to us for our own trip.

"The Association of Pleasure Craft Operators, Braunston near Rugby, Warwickshire," it read, "will send you a free brochure listing member firms and their facilities throughout Britain." Sophy had written at once to that multiple-worded organization. A prompt answer referred her to Captain L. R. Monk, head of the Maid Line Cruises. Sophy's list of pen pals was growing fast. She had already accepted an invitation, included in the literature from the British Travel Association, to become a member of the Inland Waterways Association. Membership costs one guinea and includes "a lively and informative bulletin about every second month." For all its liveliness, however, she discovered the bulletin entitled *Know Your Waterways* is not widely known; certainly not in America, and, we were both to learn, not even in England. Except for boating enthusiasts the British themselves are unaware of pleasure travel on the canals. They look on those channels as decorative features of the landscape and the towpath alongside an agreeable place on which to walk. This does not surprise me. I grew up in Chicago but never once during the years I lived there did I go on Lake Michigan in a boat, though one of the most familiar sights along its miles of shoreline is a string of harbors heavily populated with craft of every sort.

Sophy's correspondence with Captain Monk, head of the Maid Line Cruises, was spirited and revealed the captain as a man of tact and perceptiveness. Almost immediately he had introduced into his letters the suggestion of a "lad" to accompany our party. "The canal locks," he had explained, "must be operated by the navigators of the boats passing through them. Unlike the Thames they have no lockkeepers who perform that office. The men who did this in the days of heavy commercial traffic have now been diverted to maintenance of the waterways." In another letter Captain Monk did not suggest that a woman would not understand the operation of locks; he had phrased her incompetence delicately. "This operation of the locks," he wrote, "of course adds to the interest and enjoyment, providing the crew feels reasonably energetic. If there will be any males in the party, then, of course, you will be quite all right." In another letter, "If I may say so, I think a party of three ladies and two gentlemen would be far more suitable than four ladies together as some of the lock equipment on the canals is quite heavy work."

When this last suggestion had arrived we were already a party of three ladies and two gentlemen; but after considering the personnel Sophy's answering letter had included a request for a "lad."

The personnel of the *Maid Marysue* assembled that February night in Sophy's apartment had been my responsibility. In the division between Sophy and me of preparation for the trip I had taken on as a matter of course the assemblage and enlistment of a crew. There had been no foolish shilly-shallying about this arrangement; no nonsense of "you're better than I am at organizing." It had been assumed tacitly on Sophy's part that itinerary and letter writing were not to be put in my hands since I am incompetent in one and dislike the other. On the other hand there are few things I enjoy more than persuading people to go along with me on whatever undertaking has stirred my enthusiasm. I might have been the president of the Fuller Brush Company had I entered that organization. I once persuaded a group of conservative Philadelphians to learn tap dancing with me from Bill Robinson on the stage of a motion-picture theater in Asbury Park where he had offered to give public lessons free. The only time I can remember wondering if I had pushed too far was the day when overruling objections I drove companions to see how the surf would look at Barnegat Light during a hurricane and we very nearly did not return.

For the canal trip, however, I had neither coaxed nor overruled and this had both surprised and jolted me. Going over a list of friends who would be either free or compatible for traveling I had reached Arthur Kober's name one night about half past ten and had telephoned him. Author, playwright, friend—in any capacity the best possible traveling companion! I told him I had a wonderful idea. He had stimulated my zest for salesmanship, but only slightly. His voice had been a little querulous. "Now?" he had asked. "I was just going to bed. I'm undressed."

He came. A Fuller Brush man might count that an achievement but I do not; Arthur's curiosity is easily piqued. I showed him how to hold and operate the viewer for my stereo realist pictures, fed into it the series of slides I had taken of Sophy's and my cruise on the Thames two years before,* told him about the canals, promised him Sophy would know exactly where we were going so that his daughter who would be at camp could keep in touch with him, and sent him home with a copy of Dorothy Sayers' *The Nine Tailors*. This was one of the best mystery stories every written, I promised him, and had to do with bell ringers. Sophy and I had heard a weekly practice of bell ringers in Cookham and a return visit would be one of the highlights of this trip.

Two days later Arthur had telephoned me. If that was my idea of a good mystery story, he had said, apologetically, because he is a gentleman, I needn't bother to send him another, and forget about any more such literature as far as he was concerned. This was the kind of resistance I liked to hear, obstinate. I lifted my shoulders, took a deep

* *Water, Water Everywhere.*

breath waiting to let Arthur run down a little, and he said, "However, the stereo photographs were so beautiful I can't get them out of my mind. The trip sounds wonderful. I'm free since my child will be at camp so I'd love to go."

Undaunted, I had telephoned Dorothy Stickney. As the world who saw them knows, and most of the world did see them in *Life With Father,* she is the wife of Howard Lindsay. I used another approach; mine is a flexible technique. Before describing the trip I had asked her urgently, "Will you please not say anything now about what I'm going to ask you? Think it over, tell it to Howard and then let's the three of us talk about it again." I outlined the plan. When I had finished and was about to hang up she had begged me to wait. "Don't go," she said. "Do I have to think? I know right now what Howard will say. It's a dream. When do we start?" Such experiences as these can be a setback to one's talents.

Nevertheless I smiled happily at my recruits. There was Sophy, always the group leader, telling them we would board the *Maid Marysue* on the sixteenth of June at a place called Stone, and the dear silly sheep around her looked obediently at a place she indicated on the map. "It's in the Midlands," group leader elaborated for my benefit as though I cared. Two weeks later we would leave our craft at Thames Ditton "between Hampton Court and London" she told me tediously and with equally tiresome repetitiveness went over the route between for my benefit since she had noticed, she said, the first time she had outlined it, I had not been paying attention. I did not pay attention that time around either because the names held no association for me and therefore no interest. Now, however, I set them down in wistful sharp remembrance. I wish I were there this moment.

Stone is where you first see your craft and buy provisions up and down a narrow street and eat in the Crown Hotel where the paneling in the dining room is black and the food is excellent. Then comes Rugeley in Staffordshire, Lichfield in Staffordshire, too, but Nuneaton is in Warwickshire and so are Rugby and Southam. Banbury is in Oxfordshire and soon after that you leave the canals and come into the Thames at Oxford. Then there is Pangbourne in Berkshire and Cookham, too, then Windsor and at the end Thames Ditton. When I had refused to hear the names on another round and waved away the map, we talked of matters in which I could join with spirit and conviction.

Arthur requested we discuss sleeping accommodations, reminding us apologetically of his psychological involvement with too much simplicity. He wished to know how great the difference would be between, say, a stateroom on the *Queen Elizabeth* and a cabin on the *Maid Marysue*. Sophy at once produced a diagram of the canal craft and one look at this convinced Arthur the difference was too wide for his peace of mind. Dorothy and Howard also looked at each other with a wild surmise that was not a happy one. Dorothy's eyes are blue and large. I have been told sudden shock or alarm infuses into the system a jolt of adrenalin. I think in Dorothy's chemistry it produces a sort of belladonna. From her optic reaction and expansion it was apparent Dorothy had received a jolt, although the only thing she said was, "Oh my!"

11

In the years I have known the Lindsays I have come to recognize when Howard pulls his mustache in staccato jerks he is a passenger pulling the emergency cord to stop the train. He had not spoken but he was stopping the train when Sophy proposed astutely, "How would it be if we tied up each night near a village and slept at an inn? I could write for accommodations." The Lindsays and Kober relaxed, sighed and smiled happily. Howard said, "Wonderful idea," let go his emergency cord and Sophy's hair rose.

I cannot explain this phenomenon. It occurs when Sophy is pleased, triumphant and executive. I think it improbable that adrenalin and belladonna converge on her scalp but I do assert that though running the hands through one's hair is a common gesture in moments of tension, I have never seen Sophy do this. Nevertheless the evidence that she is experiencing triumph or a crisis of some sort is that her hair, short and curly as it is normally, leaves its accustomed waves and stands upright. "I will write," she repeated happily. "Mr. Beer is the man for this, I think." The name was unknown to us, and she explained, "He's in the British Transport Commission of the British Transport Waterways," and it was obvious she enjoyed the multiplicity of his title. "I've already had a letter from him."

While she daydreamed happily of the letter-writing involved in the plan she had proposed, a different inn in a different village every night and accommodations for all of us in each, I introduced the subject of clothes and general equipment. This is a topic to which Sophy begrudges attention. "Warm," she said, "raincoats certainly," and went back to her daydreams. I would not be put off by any such generalization.

"This is something I feel strongly about," I told the others. Having contributed nothing to the plans up to this point nor been asked to contribute, and also because this was a matter of concern to me, I was doubly emphatic. "Whatever we wear on board—" I urged, "and slacks are imperative, a skirt can catch on a piece of equipment and throw you—but I beg that we put on conventional, inconspicuous clothes whenever we leave the boat. If there is one thing I abominate it's the sight of Americans abroad swinging along in loud patterned sport shirts, women in shorts or slacks, and sandals with nothing but a sole and a thong between two toes. I think it's disgusting. I know it won't be easy," I continued persuasively. "We'll have to get out of our boat clothes and into others, take overnight things with us to the inns and change again when we come back to the boat in the morning, and maybe you think it's too much of a fuss." I paused to allow dispute. Stickney, Lindsay and Kober spoke almost simultaneously. "You're absolutely right" was the gist of their chorus. "I don't care how much trouble it is. If the cabin space is small we'll change in shifts." I have never before encountered a group with such maddeningly little sales resistance.

Complications are as exhilarating to Sophy as resistance is to me. In my family things happen before you can say "Jack Robinson." In Sophy's they occur before you can say "knife" and in that much less time she was at her desk making new pen friends and crossing off the complications.

Mr. Beer, of the British Transport Commission of the

British Transport Waterways, submitted an itinerary of hotels and inns at which we could stop. Someone else made reservations at each of these places, another spate of letters provided the assurance of a car to take us night and morning from and to our boat. Mr. Turbayne, of the British Travel Association in New York, sent cables on our behalf to England, and pamphlets to Sophy about the beauties in Wales and Scotland. The brother of an English friend of the Lindsays revealed himself a canal enthusiast and sent charts and invaluable data. We came even to the notice of the Shah of the British Transport Waterways, Major General Sir Reginald Kerr, K.B.E., C.B., M.C., M.Inst.T. The only arrival I can think of awaited with comparable anticipation was Lindbergh's descent on Paris. We were not such pioneers as that adventurer. Other Americans have certainly cruised the British Inland Waterways, but considering the attention focused on our trip, those others must have traveled unobtrusively. We were not obtrusive intentionally. It is just that Sophy plans thoroughly and widely. Even she, however, did not forehandedly include a photographer and reporter from *Life* magazine. They surprised her and that is not an easy thing to do.

I was surprised when Sophy told me she had engaged a converted canal boat for two weeks, from May twenty-fifth to June the eighth, on which she and I would go into Wales. Since the others of our prospective party could not join us so early as that, it would give an opportunity to run a sort of trial heat, was her explanation.

I would never recommend Sophy to the Fuller Brush Company. She has known me for more than thirty years

14

and yet she told me as a persuasive inducement this excursion would include crossing Telford's great aqueduct at Pontcysyllte, 1,007 feet long and 121 feet high, and going through the Harecastle Tunnel, 2,919 yards long. and she read from *Know Your Waterways:* "This is still an adventurous experience. One adventurous element is that the tunnel is much lower in the center than at each end. There is a towpath through but again it is under water in the center," as though a tunnel nearly a mile long were not horrifying enough without a sag in the middle.

Sophy has seen me motoring on mountain roads in Greece with my hands like Venetian blinds before my face. She knows we had scarcely started a descent to the catacombs beneath the baths of Caracalla in Rome when I had left her and my other companions and made for the surface again on the gallop. Therefore, I count it no selling accomplishment of hers when I said I would go on a cruise that would include an aqueduct and a tunnel. I have long had a yearning to see Wales, but my private reservations were that somehow or other I would skirt the aqueduct, and remain above the tunnel.

I forestalled whatever other surprises Sophy may have been brewing in the back of her mind or at her desk by making a few plans of my own and announcing them to her and the rest of the crew at a subsequent meeting. We met frequently that month in order to catch up on and hear reports of our group leader's correspondence. Bulletins from the rest of us were of a more trivial nature. I had found a place where slacks could be made at no more cost than those available in shops but with considerably more concessions to the deviations that middle age brings to standard sizes. At the same place I had also come upon lightweight nylon jackets that were water repellent. I advocated strongly, though gloomily, the purchase of this sort of equipment. Undoubtedly it would rain most of the time in England, I prophesied. Sophy was stern about keeping the bulk of equipment as low as possible considering the restrictions of space, and each time she stressed this she thumped with a pencil the diagram of the *Maid Marysue*. Our theme, as the fashion reporters call each season's trend, was warmth. "England is cold," Howard said, "and so are boats. So a boat in England is bound to be very cold."

At this meeting Sophy told the others her surprise for me of our trip to Wales, emphasizing her thoughtfulness in paving the way and ironing out all difficulties before the others should arrive. They were touched by such solicitude, and mindful that the aqueduct and tunnel were in the path of our trip, not theirs, I considered their gratitude thoroughly warranted.

My own surprise brought nothing like such glowing commendation when I announced it. The interest it aroused was more perfunctory than warm, I felt, though I was almost feverish with anticipation. I had been in communication, I told them, with my stepmother in California. I had suggested she and I go to Italy in April, meet my daughter and son-in-law, who would fly down from Paris where they were living, have a holiday together showing them Italy for their first time, go back with them to Paris for what in Indiana we call a "visit" with them and my grandchildren. I would leave my stepmother there for a longer stay, come to England and join Sophy for that inspired jaunt of hers. I was already feeling somewhat deflated when I shared this program with the crew of the *Maid Marysue* because Achsah, my stepmother, had followed their pattern and accepted immediately without so much as a gasp of resistance my proposal of our trip together. Therefore, when I had, as an immediate answer to a first suggestion, a letter from Madame Pandit saying she would be delighted to join Sophy and me for part of our cruise in Wales, I relegated salesmanship to the Lost Arts. Sophy's and my friendship with India's High Commissioner to England dates back to the early days of the UN and becomes the more affectionately rooted by frequent visits back and forth and always the great pleasure of her company. This letter of acceptance included an insistence that Sophy and I stay with her in London before starting the cruise.

The crew came to see Achsah and me off on the *Queen Frederica* the morning of April 24th. This ship was the one on which three close friends, including Sophy, and I had gone to Greece two years before.* The selection of this vessel to take Achsah and me as far as Naples was an expression of an idiosyncrasy of mine. Just as I like to return to plays I have enjoyed, my pleasure in them mounting with each succeeding visit, I like to touch the places I have loved before going on to new ones. Rome, Florence, Venice, Paris and the *Queen Frederica* are in this category. I consider the *Queen Frederica* the pleasantest ship on which I have traveled. Sophy shares my conviction. The sight of our accommodations, the very

* *Water, Water Everywhere.*

ones she and I had occupied on the preceding trip, and of the stewardess, Yolanda, who had taken care of us, so swamped her with nostalgia she was for a moment or two of a mind to take cover in a lifeboat and remain there until we were well at sea. However, when a gong and a summons of "Passengers ashore" sounded in the corridor she abandoned her wild plan and reluctantly accompanied Dorothy, Howard and Arthur down the gangplank.

Mercifully our departing guests were experienced travelers. They know the exasperation to the ones on board of waiting until the ship actually sails, exchanging idiotic arm waving and foolish messages that could have been given in the cabin and are impossible to hear from the dock. At the instant of their departure Achsah and I left the deck purposefully. When I see the dock seemingly moving away from me I have a hysterical determination to get back to it somehow. I count myself a dolt for having got on something that is taking me away from my dear ones. Though I am going to see one daughter I am leaving another behind, and familiar places and things I haven't done. I know now the way to meet this panic is to allow myself to look at the skyline of New York only as I approach it, never when I am quitting it. Achsah and I went to our staterooms.

CHAPTER TWO

ON SATURDAY, the 25th of May, at about noon, Sophy and I boarded a train at Euston Station in London. As children say in games we were getting warmer, warmer. The *Venturer* was waiting for us on the Trent and Mersey Canal at Stone. I had traveled such a wide circumference around this spot and so much had happened since the time it had been marked on the map I felt a kinship, as I climbed into the railway carriage, with a child who, blindfolded, is whirled around three times and then instructed to pin the tail on the donkey. I was bewildered, apprehensive lest I miss the mark, and excited by the anticipation of actually touching the goal.

Three days earlier Sophy and I had arrived within a few hours of each other at the Indian Embassy in London. Sophy had flown from New York, I had come from Paris. Madame Pandit, India's High Commissioner and decisive executive, had put me to bed because I had a bad cold. I marvel at Madame Pandit's breadth of knowledge, and her administrative ability. I recognize these qualities and accord them my deepest honor and respect untouched by a personal sense of inadequacy and certainly not envy. I know and am resigned to my own limitations, recognizing how small the frame is that contains my range of ability; but I take count of Madame Pandit's qualities as a hostess with ruefulness and something close to despair. In my house I welcome guests with pleasure and enthusiasm. I am concerned they should be comfortable but though my eyesight is normal I do not see in the container hanging on the side of the bathtub an almost transparent wisp of soap laid crosswise in order not to slip through the bars of the soap dish. I do not notice that the last time the vacuum cleaner was used the floor plug for the bed lamp was not replaced. The visitor to this chamber of omissions learns of these inadequacies by losing the soap and by finding she cannot read in bed until she restores the connection after an exploratory tour on all fours along the baseboard.

Such oversights will never be discovered in the guest room of any house Madame Pandit occupies. Whatever the size of her staff, whatever the bulk of her outside obligations she personally views the guest-room landscape o'er, with a penetrating eye for details. She adds warmth and solicitude together with an unresistible authority that had put me to bed and only a few minutes later beside me hot tea and toast, a bunch of grapes and a book she thought I would enjoy. While I had fumed there in luxury she had taken Sophy on a round of fascinating activities.

On the train with Sophy I caught up with these vicariously. I heard with twinges of envy and occasional winces of resentment about a reception for the Nigerian Premier just arrived in London and how lavishly beautiful it was; a private showing of a film on Ghana's independence at which all the diplomatic corps was present; a reception in Festival Hall for the Governor General of Ghana and his wife. Sophy emphasized the unforgettable sight of the blending of top British and African representatives with missionaries and diplomats of other countries. The thing, she said, that impressed her particularly was the eagerness of all the white-skinned people to show their realization of the importance of this occasion celebrating the recent independence of Ghana. I thought she was a little more impressed by the champagne and plovers' eggs.

Though I had been visited conscientiously and solicitously by Sophy and our hostess during brief stops on this sparkling merry-go-round I had been urged threateningly not to use my voice during their calls. It was true my cold had induced a severe case of laryngitis; nevertheless the frustration of being neither able nor allowed to speak was far more painful to me than any chest or head discomfort. I compensated for my frustration by imposing on Sophy during the train ride a detailed account of my own activities from the time she had waved me off on the *Queen Frederica* to her wave of greeting to me from the landing of the stairway of the Indian Embassy as I came through the door, six weeks later.

I told her of our voyage on that favorite ship, and of our belated landing at Naples delayed by a heavy storm in the first days of the voyage. A further delay in Naples of a wearisome hour from half past twelve to half past one in the morning had balked us because a customs official, a very young man, had been so pleasurably provoked by the sight of the movie projector I was bringing to my son-in-law he had summoned a friend. Together they had examined with happy cries every bolt and screw on the machine, removing it first by tearing apart its wrappings. When at the end of an hour the projector was restored to me, clumsily enveloped in a newspaper, its outline had looked for all the world like a chamber pot in my arms.

We had traveled all night reaching Rome at sunrise. Achsah and I had slept intermittently, but the daylight had awakened us, and, I told Sophy, Achsah and I had thanked aloud whatever Greek gods might have chastised the *Queen Frederica* by a storm at sea. By this subduing of her schedule we had had our first sight of Rome at the moment when Apollo rode into our sky. The clouds were pink shells and pointing up at them like a fat thumb was the dome of St. Peter's, the widespread hand of the city beneath and around it. Let Sophy remember the Nigerians, I told her, in their vivid robes; I would never forget Rome at sunrise.

I pursued my chronicle relentlessly. I took Sophy, figuratively, with Achsah and me to the rapturous reunion with my daughter; our days in Rome and our discovery that my daughter's pregnancy was to be a red carpet for us that would lead us to the best table in any restaurant, and immediate service everywhere, given with solicitude frequently expressed by an affectionate pat on her rump and a murmured congratulation. We had not permitted her to stand aside for her elders. Within a few moments on our first excursion we had stepped behind; following her leadership our every arrival had been a triumphant entry. I admit an expectant mother is an item of traveling equipment not easily come by, but for getting the best out of a trip there is nothing comparable to it.

From Rome we had gone to Florence and I forced on Sophy very nearly every step of the way. There my son-in-law had joined us and apart from the familiar and loved sights we visited, I told her, the memory I shall carry from now on is the touchingly absurd image of my daughter endeavoring over a large natural obstacle to press her face against shop windows whose contents had attracted her to an almost hysterical rapture.

The ancient mariner did not hold the wedding guest with more firmness than I forced Sophy to attend my recital of our progress from Florence to Venice and the experience there of deep and thorough contentment that settles in when people you love respond with like joyousness to a loved place. Venice to Paris and a fatuous meeting, expressed in terms of idiotic idolatry, with two grandchildren, and finally the parting with my family. Then the last lap of the trip complete with cold, due to the chilly dampness of Paris after the sunny warmth of Italy. Finally I released Sophy at the end of my story and she proposed lunch. I think she was tired.

Not long after lunch we reached Stone. We had left the train at Stafford and been met there by two men from the British Waterways, one driving a taxi, the other a pickup truck. The truck, it was explained, was for our luggage and over-all equipment. Since our over-all equipment was contained in two suitcases apiece, the truck had been superfluous and the men were disconcerted. We mollified them by transferring to their care the considerable number of coats each of us carried, short, long and rain. I do not know what they had expected us to bring. Even the British traveling today leave behind their portable bathtubs and other standard pieces that were once indispensable accompaniments to any trip. But it was obvious these two couriers had expected considerably more than the modest equipment handed over to them.

It is perhaps ten miles from Stafford to Stone. It seemed longer to me, paradoxically, because our driver drove very fast, especially around curves or when passing a vehicle at the moment when another was bearing down on us from the opposite direction, each one of these to my American eye on the wrong side of the road.

The Crown Hotel in Stone is on the curving, narrow main street of the town. We discovered its charm later. On our arrival I noticed nothing about it except the identifying sign swinging above the door. By this time as in the children's game we were no longer warm, we were hot, and no children playing were ever more feverish than we. We signed the register, fidgeted with impatience at the tranquil tempo of the lady clerk in finding the key to our room, insistence on summoning the landlord for introductions, and his measured pace as he conducted us to our quarters. But on this, to us, interminable passage, he gave directions for finding the canal and our boat. They were simple and the place close at hand.

The moment our luggage was deposited we left our guide unceremoniously, and the hotel. A footpath around the side of the inn, through a meadow, past a coalyard where children were playing, brought us to the canal and the very spot where the *Venturer* was moored. I am old enough, God and my birth certificate know, to be dismally aware of how frequently realization falls short of anticipation, but one exception to this rule can restore my chronic optimism. The *Venturer* was everything an exception should be, bright, gay and unreasonable. I am not a yachtsman but that is not a requirement for seeing boats, and over the years I have looked at a good number of craft; but never has one come to my eye remotely resembling the object of Sophy's and my incredulous acknowledgment that this was what we had planned so long to reach.

We had read that barges are called Narrow Boats but we had to see one to realize when they say narrow they mean less than seven feet across, and that is not wide. We knew from Sophy's correspondence the sort of Narrow Boat on which we would travel was one that had been converted to a "pleasure craft" but in the mind's eye we had not seen that converting would be cutting a seventy-foot commercial barge in half, then adding an additional ten feet at the stern for engine and cabin space. We had not visualized in the bow, a deck, if it could be called that, large enough to hold two people, possibly three, standing wedged close together, or one seated. The deck in the stern looked more like a back porch than anything nautical. It included a built-in bench following the curve of the boat, and in the center a stout, thick rod as high as a man's armpit and looking far more like an elongated pump handle than a tiller. Wildly as my imagination can run it had not suggested to me a cabin superstructure enclosed and roofed. This strain in the mongrel vessel was definitely houseboat. Double, swinging doors at either end were painted in a series of panels. These alternated from a garland of vivid flowers in yellow, red and green to a landscape of meadow and stream dominated by a castle lavishly and preposterously turreted. I noticed the windows of the superstructure—and though they were small they numbered at least six on each side—were hung in flowered chintz. I realized the feeling of being in a child's game was justified. Now we were going to "play house."

Two men were working on the pump handle and the flooring of the back porch was up revealing an engine. Sophy and I, staring at the playhouse, had not exchanged a word, but one of the men looking up caught sight of us. "Good afternoon," he said and nudged his companion. They both stepped on shore immediately, one of them introducing himself as Mr. Wyatt, owner of the boatyard and one of Sophy's pen pals. They were checking the engine, he said, but if we would like to see the interior we could enter from the bow. Since from February until this moment in May I had been wondering at least once a day how a converted barge would look outside and in, I would have liked to shout to him and the surrounding countryside, "Yes, I would like to see the inside of a boat I've traveled three thousand miles to board," but "restraint" is the watchword for an American in England and so I answered softly, "Thank you very much," and hearing myself knew I had picked up the germ to which I am the most susceptible.

There is no need for me to state, though I do it frequently, I was born in the Middle West. My speech is sufficient herald of this news. It accompanies me through whatever country I travel but it leaves me on British soil. There I am so vulnerable I am immediately invaded by that country's speech and accent. My aggressive r's are routed, and my broad, flat a's shrunk to half their native breadth. Sophy on the other hand carries with her an immunity that comes of being born in Philadelphia, where change is not acceptable. She heard me, however, and groaned. "You've caught it already," she said, "I might have known," and followed Mr. Wyatt.

"Mind the low door and the steps when you come in," he called back.

"Right," I answered and Sophy groaned again.

Perhaps that is why I did not talk while we examined the interior, or perhaps it was the silence of satisfaction at what I saw. I only remember distinctly not saying anything because those occasions for me are infrequent. Sophy chattered about the route we would take, the potential speed of our boat and other foolish details that impressed Mr. Wyatt.

From the bow we ducked through a pair of low doors, went down two steps and were in a cabin with a bunk on either side and windows above. There were drawers under each bunk, too, and a thin wardrobe at the far end of the room. The beds were covered to match a row of pillows under the windows so that by day these were couches on which to sit. A door, painted in garlands, opened to the center cabin, the largest. This was equipped as sitting room, dining room, kitchen and single bedroom. The couch here was obviously a sleeping bunk at night. There were two armchairs and I saw other folding chairs under the bunk. A hinged table was folded against the wall. Obviously this was to be let down when a meal was ready. The meal could be prepared on a small but adequate stove that included even an oven. Next the stove was a sink with a shelf and two little windows above it. Whatever details of the *Venturer*'s equipment may fade from my memory

27

those little windows will remain clear and exasperating. They opened out, but I did not know on that first day of happy inspection they must be closed each time we went under a bridge or through a lock because the channel there would be so narrow as to shatter them against the sides of lock or bridge. I had not learned, either, that among the other menial tasks assigned to me would be the office of window closer. Nor could I foresee on that afternoon when our barge slapped softly against the wall of the canal as we walked back and forth, I would almost invariably be in the bow when the alarm reached me that a bridge or lock was at hand; and that I would not walk, as we were leisurely sauntering on that inspection tour, but run. At this pace, with monotonous regularity, I would crack my head against the low door from the bow and reel from there to those wretched windows above the sink.

The cabin in the stern was larger than the one in the bow and was evidently the master bedroom because the bathroom that included wash basin and toilet was next door to it. The location was not ideal. Its proximity to the operation and operator of the boat was embarrassingly conspicuous. We did not think of this at first sight and later became so accustomed we ceased to think of it at all.

We visited next Mr. Wyatt's office, only a few yards beyond the *Venturer*'s mooring, and I suppose because its location was on the very brink of the canal the wooden building was on high stilts. In the office we signed papers, checked supplies of linen, blankets, towels, silver, etc. The bookkeeper-cashier was Mr. Wyatt's mother and when we had finished our business she asked if we would like to see where she lived. She assured us it was not far away: a characteristically British understatement. Mrs. Wyatt lived in a houseboat moored beside the office. When we entered we were introduced to a friend who had dropped by for tea. Our arrival had interrupted them but the kettle was bubbling on the stove, the tea things were out. We could not accept the hostess's invitation to join them because we had other errands but even had we stayed I doubt I would have lost my sense of incongruity in visiting a small charming country cottage that floated on the water.

Returning the way we had come we paused a moment in the coalyard to see if we could identify a game the children were playing with flat stones. It was not difficult. Each of us had once played Ducks and Drakes, Sophy in Pennsylvania and I in Indiana, and by this common denominator in Staffordshire, England, we were neighbors. Looking back at the canal, however, I sensed the first faint awareness that people living there were not neighbors to folk from Indiana nor Pennsylvania nor even the village of Stone across the meadow from where we stood. I had not noticed before, because the sight of the *Venturer* had drawn my whole attention, a number of boats drawn up in single file along the bank within my view. I saw a man step ashore from one of these, walk past two others and at the third, knock on one of its windows and call out, "Oy, Bill?" and a man's voice answered from inside, "Aye, coom in." A caller, I thought, dropping in for tea like the guest on Mrs. Wyatt's boat and probably she had come from another craft, not from the town. These were water people, and no playground nor any other *ground* could create for them, by familiarity, a neighborhood.

"I think we had better go," Sophy said, "we have so

much to do." I followed her abstractedly, preoccupied by an intoxicating fantasy of someone knocking on the window of the *Venturer* and my calling out an invitation to come in for a "spot" of tea, and the visitor assuming casually, "You're water people, aren't you?" and my answering as I ruthlessly scythed out of existence the cornfields of Indiana, "Oh, yes indeed, out of Stone in Staffordshire." Restraint would be my watchword. I would not overdo my kinship with barge society, but I would establish it, with perhaps even a Midlands accent.

There is no fantasy about shopping in Stone. Shopping there, we were to find, is like shopping in any of the other English towns in which we bought provisions, but provides no kinship with any town at home. The British common denominator is inconvenience. We Americans are pampered housekeepers, pushing a cart through a supermarket and dropping into it breakfast food, vegetables, milk and butter, meat or fish, Kleenex and cigarettes. When we have checked off every item on our shopping list we pause at a counter, pay for what we have bought, see it all put into a beautiful, stout paper container and carried to our car. It is not like that in England, my dears. Staples are in one shop but nothing is provided there in which to put them.

"Have you no container?" the first shopkeeper we visited inquired incredulously and then I knew why every woman we passed carried suspended over one arm a long, limp band of woven string with handles. We admitted apologetically we had no container.

The British have patience far beyond the quota in the temperament of other people! I do not know whether this

is an inherent quality, or developed by trials and an accustomedness to the inadequacy of things, and of Americans. The shopkeeper was patient with us. He wrapped our purchases in bits of paper he had saved from packages delivered to him. He had no string, and soon after we had left him our parcels began to open. A light breeze blew the flapping ends of mine across the lower part of my face in tantalizing fashion, causing me agonizedly to want to sneeze.

Each of us bought a string bag at the first shop that carried them, though this was not the first shop we visited. Nothing we required was in the first shop at which we made inquiries, and no matter which side of the street we tried first, what we needed was across the way. A busy way, crowded with trucks, "lorries" I was already saying, passenger cars, bicycles, motor bikes and other women shoppers like us, except most of these pushed a pram and herded three or four toddling stragglers.

Butter and eggs are under one roof but milk and cream are not there, any more than lettuce is to be purchased where salt and vinegar are for sale. Olive oil is purchased at the chemist's. Of course, bread is not at any of these places. It is at the baker's though there are adventurers among these who will include cakes and pastries. Meat, of course, is at the butcher's. "But whatever would make you think," that gentleman inquired benevolently, "that we would have chicken? Chicken is poultry. Across the way and up the street." I had not wanted chicken nor anything else that required so much attention. On a cruise there would be views I would prefer to the inside of an oven or broiler, but I was curious to learn how far this subdivision of supplies was stretched. Also I wanted an excuse to stand still for a few minutes. For an hour we had been trudging this zigzag shopping course. My legs ached and, because I had shifted the bag from one to the other, both arms were numb. Butter, bread, milk, eggs, cheese, salt, pepper, sugar, coffee, tea. It was a list that at home could have been filled in a quarter of an hour within an area of a hundred or so paces. We were on our second hour and had made at least three laps around the course on this trial-and-error run.

Our major error had been an idea—mine—that we could purchase an ice bucket, the sort of receptacle on every cocktail tray across America. That was as moonstruck a flight of fancy as ever entered an addled pate. In the first shop where I made my naïve inquiry I met total lack of comprehension and a mistrustful scrutiny that backed me out of the door again in a hurry to rejoin Sophy. Sophy will solicit any information as long as the solicitation can be made in writing. If it must be ascertained verbally she invariably remains on the sidewalk.

Following directions from the next shopkeeper I visited, we found the goal suggested was an establishment that sold pottery. I was shown vases, bowls and platters. I dare say to this merchant my suggestion of preserving ice was as idiotic to him as his was to me of a tasteful arrangement of cubes in one of the vases as a table decoration. To ask where I could buy an ice bucket had been my first mistake. To think I knew where one could be bought was my second. My third was to inquire where I might find a hardware store.

In the opinion of the shopkeepers I had already visited I was an eccentric. This was obvious in the manner of their response, soothing but wary. My use of the phrase "hardware store," a phrase made up of English words but, to their ears, heterogeneously assembled and without any meaning, provoked such a mistrustful silence from the personnel of the bakery that with a silly smile and a sickly apology, I do not know for what, I again rejoined Sophy on the sidewalk. I had no solace from her, but I had not expected it. Next to asking people questions face to face, Sophy dislikes being halted in the swift completion of her appointed rounds. I like punctuation in my prose and my activities, Sophy prefers to go straight through to the period at the end of the sentence or errand. She considered an ice bucket an interruption. Furthermore she was embarrassed, she said, by the way people inside watched me leave the shop. It was apparent to her even on the street side of the window, they considered me outlandish. She regretted being associated with me under their observation. She counted their appraisal of me justifiable, considering, she said, most English people have very little use for ice in the first place, so why would they want to keep it? She added a suggestion that since I was so quick to take on an English accent I might do well to learn an English vocabulary and not throw about such foreign phrases as "hardware store."

I had agreed to give up the search and the phrase but the butcher was so patient with my ignorance of where poultry was to be found I ventured one more try. Across Sophy's look of astonished outrage as one who has been betrayed, I asked that kind man if he could suggest a place where we might find a receptacle in which ice might be preserved. This was a new technique. I did not say "ice

34

bucket" nor "hardware store." Furthermore I anticipated his appraisal by identifying myself—out of kindness or intimidation I did not include Sophy—as an American with a foolish eccentricity of liking cold drinks. I shook my head deprecatingly at my own folly. I thought he was going to pat my head as he leaned over the counter toward me, and Sophy jumped aside nervously. But his large red hand reached beyond my face and pointed toward the street. "Have ye tried the ironmonger's across the way?" he asked.

In the Midlands they say "noo" and I heard myself say it. "Noo," I answered, "I halven't and I thank ye very much."

"Oh my God" was what I heard Sophy mutter.

When I was a child in Muncie, Indiana, a ragged and dirty old man used to drive a wagon past our house about once a week. Over the top was strung a row of bells that jangled. Above this noise the driver called frequently, "Old iron, old iron."

Until this moment I had thought that man and others like him were ironmongers and it would not have occurred to me to rummage for an ice bucket in the contents of their wagons.

The merchandise in the establishment of the ironmonger in Stone was even more heterogeneous than the assortment I had glimpsed over the rim of the traveling carts in Muncie, though it was of a vastly superior quality. Nevertheless it did not include an ice bucket. The shop owner was sympathetic and obliging. He brought out a number of objects he thought might do, blowing dust off each one before setting it on the counter before us. The dustiest

35

of all was a small thermos bottle that took him some time to discover. He hadn't seen it, he said, "in donkey's years," and conveyed to us his bewilderment at having stocked it in the first place. Brimming, it might have held two cups of liquid, but the neck was too small to allow the insertion of any but crushed ice. He had been so willing, however, and so uncritical of my eccentricity I could not bear to leave without making a purchase. That is why Sophy and I returned to the inn swinging between us a large pail of plastic in bright yellow.

"We can use it for garbage," Sophy decided. "Only in that color it will be hard to keep out of Arthur's sight."

CHAPTER THREE

A MAN was standing by the *Venturer* when Sophy and I reached the canal at about nine o'clock the following morning. He was close to six feet tall. His face and hands were deeply tanned though his cheeks were ruddy as a Jonathan apple. Some of his black hair was noticeably absent from forehead to very nearly the crown of his head, and though he was not fat an over-all stockiness was a familiar evidence that middle age had moved into the original frame. He watched our approach with a friendly but rather shy curiosity and while I was thinking I like the straightforward unfurtive scrutiny of his brown eyes and wondering who he was, Mr. Wyatt came along, introduced and identified the stranger. The identification came as something of a surprise. "This is Mr. Walley," Mr. Wyatt told us. "He is the lad engaged for your cruise." We learned later the lad had sometime previously celebrated his fiftieth birthday, but even at the moment of introduction I realized "lad" was a term to add to my English vocabulary. "Lad" denoted evidently an occupation, a usage something like our Western Union "boy." Mr. Walley moved from the boat immediately to shake hands and to take over some of our equipment. Another man approached us from the office and was introduced by Mr. Wyatt. He was Mr. Lloyd of the Inland Waterways Association and had come to welcome us to the canals.

Our arrival at the dock had been incongruously like pictures I have seen of a safari. Our bearers, not in the least resembling African natives, were porters from the hotel and some unidentified men, but they had walked in single file behind us across the meadow and through the coalyard, carrying our bags and the accumulation of the previous day's shopping. A little boy who had probably got himself into the procession by persuasion was the calliope of the parade. He whistled and swung from one hand the yellow plastic bucket.

While we were still in formation I noticed a small group of people not far from the *Venturer,* three or four men and two women I think. I noticed them because they were obviously noticing us and while Mr. Walley was directing and assisting the transfer of our "traps," as he called them, to the boat, the group approached. Sophy evidently thought this was another cruising party and hailed them with the supposition they were starting out like us, and didn't we have a beautiful, sunny day? The members of this party corrected her and my impression. They were not going anywhere, they separately told us, and identified themselves as representatives of the local paper. They had assembled because word had got around Americans were going to travel the canals and such a thing had never been heard of, at least not from this depot. They would like a photograph and a statement of how we had come to do such an unlikely thing. The photograph was considerably easier to achieve than the statement. How could we explain briefly, Sophy and I asked each other in low tones as we were being posed, the devious way that had brought us here? We compromised with the tried if not true statement we had always longed to explore this part of England. They apparently were nonplussed. One woman phrased their doubt neatly. "You've come all the way across the Atlantic Ocean to go on a canal?" she asked. We admitted this and I think both of us felt we owed the folk at home an apology for providing one more reason to look on Americans as capricious will- o'-the-wisps.

Mr. Walley stood in the stern at the pump handle. Everything was aboard, he told us, and whenever we were ready we could take off. Sophy promptly spanned the gap from shore to bow with a long and spirited leap. I went to the stern and acknowledged gratefully the hand of Mr. Walley to pull me in and the boost behind from Mr. Wyatt to get me up and over.

Our send-off was, in a modest way, spectacular. The safari attendants had waited even after they had been paid, and joined with the newspaper group. Even Mr. Wyatt's mother came out of the office, ran down the steps and added her wave, good-by, and good luck to the chorus.

We had gone only a few yards and I was still responding with arm and voice when we disappeared out of sight of everything into a tunnel. I was appalled and outraged. If my lack of knowledge of geography and Sophy's secretiveness had conspired to get me into the tunnel that she had read about and I had craftily determined to avoid, thinking it a crisis to be reached days later, I would leave the *Venturer* at once. If the water there were so deep as to require swimming, the distance back to the waving well-wishers was within my capacity of fifty strokes and, landing, I could reassure the group there were some Americans who were by nature stay-at-homes.

It was not a tunnel at all. It was a kind of roofed-over shed with water in a channel beneath. This allowed us to turn in, back out and head in the opposite direction from the way in which the boat had previously pointed. No one, namely Sophy, had thought to tell me in which direction our itinerary was charted. My relief at being in the open again outweighed my discomfiture at being turned around without warning, and I resumed my farewell gestures to the still-active assemblage on shore.

Sophy was in the bow and I in the stern when we cast off, but we met midship soon after and shook hands in mutual congratulation; this was IT and we were here; a boat called the *Venturer,* manned by a lad named Mr. Walley, was at this very moment carrying us on the Mersey Trent Canal through Staffordshire. We corroborated our departure from everything familiar by shedding our town clothes and climbing into slacks, a garment I had not worn since the day I left size 12.

It was not easy to move about inside the cabin that on the day before had seemed commodious. Accumulation of our equipment in a heap had reduced the area considerably. Nevertheless we decided this was not the time for such trivia as straightening up and putting away, and our decision was clinched by a shout from Mr. Walley that we were approaching a lock. This announcement was as great a surprise to me as my recent immersion in the tunnel. Perhaps I am easily surprised, but I had somehow thought a lock was something come upon gradually and observable from a considerable distance. Actually this was not idle fancy on my part. When we had cruised on the Thames we had been warned by conspicuous signposts we were approaching a lock and had begun to make preparations. Sophy, the captain, had slowed down and watched for a mooring post should we find the gates locked and have to wait outside for their opening. I, the ignominious "decky," had gathered in my hands the rope with which, always futilely, I would endeavor to lasso that post. Here there was neither anticipation nor preparation. Mr. Walley called, "Coming to a lock," and by the time on the double we had reached his side we were at the entrance. It did not in any way resemble those approaches with which I had become familiar on the Thames: a long passageway with solid stone walls on either side; a broad coping along the top reached by a flight of stone steps; beyond the coping green lawn and a charming, well-kept garden that adjoined a lockkeeper's cottage; ahead, massive barriers that were the lock gates. The lockkeeper himself and frequently his wife too would be waiting our arrival and, though they did not expect it, the wild fling of the rope from my hands in a wayward direction, and an equally wild appeal from me for one of them to catch and secure it.

The only indications of a lock here were stone walls on either side of a narrow passage, and ahead two long poles of rough wood attached to an upright base.

"We're in the pound," Mr. Walley explained. "Those are the lock gates. The ones beyond will be closed." I could not have imagined anything more unlike the lock gates on the Thames than these. On the river the gates had been solid doors, looming high above our heads. These were like the barriers at a railway crossing. They were open now and flat against either bank, scarcely noticeable as we passed. A few yards further on we reached the second gate. This was closed. We were scarcely moving now and as we nosed up to the far barrier Mr. Walley jumped from the boat carrying what looked like the crank my grandfather used to start his Haynes automobile. He walked back to the gates behind, pushed against one of the poles and the two swung closed. This done he fitted his crank over a sort of bolt and began turning, at first with difficulty then more easily. He came back and as he passed us on the way to the far gate he called, "I've dropped the paddles behind, noo I'll raise the ones ahead to let in the water to level us." He walked across the gates on the side away from us. I saw later that each gate has a narrow ledge someone else, not I, might walk on. Arriving at the other side he repeated his cranking exercise and at that instant Sophy and I, who had been watching intently what was going on, turned to each other and simultaneously thanked Providence aloud that a "lad" was with us. We turned back to see what the lad grown so dear in the last minute would do next. He did nothing for the time it might have taken us to count to a hundred slowly, then he put both hands against the gate and began to push. It resisted him at first, and he waited, then tried again. This time the gate yielded easily. Mr. Walley came back along the ledge. By now there was a considerable gap in the middle. He leaped across this gap, and picturing myself in such a breach, I very nearly sank to my knees from weakness at the thought, and in thanksgiving that such aerial, let along muscular work had not been required of me. Our lad returned to the boat; the crank was hanging down his back. At the moment he had finished raising the second paddle, whatever that meant, I had seen him hook the handle inside his coat collar. As he jumped aboard he removed it and put it under the bench in the stern. "You never want to lay the windlass down," he advised us, "else you can go off without it and then you are in trouble." Sophy nodded a solemn agreement to this. My own unspoken response was that I never wanted to pick it up.

The gates were wide open now. The canal stretched before us. We were on our way again.

Somewhere in that operation Mr. Walley had dropped the paddles back into their original place. I know this was accompanied by a rattle of chains and later I knew he was as put out as his equable nature allowed when he discovered preceding voyagers had neglected to do this. I knew from our former cruise, once we were in the lock the gates would be closed behind us, the ones before us being already shut. Then, if the terrain ahead required one to be lifted to its level, water would be let in to lift us. If a down grade were ahead, water would be released to lower us to the required level. Only on the canals are the levels achieved by raising a section of each gate (called the "paddle" because of its shape) with a windlass, and dropping or closing it when this level has been achieved. I shall always remember the sensation of being raised, or lowered from beneath, as a dentist chair operates. I shall hear the sound of the water—the first gush, strong as when a fire hydrant is turned on; then the heavy, steady but hollow roar as the cavity fills. I shall smell, too, the damp walls on either side and feel their chill. I was almost invariably at a window in the galley during the operation.

I took over that stand soon after we had left the lock. I have only myself to blame for reaching it so early. I take a deplorable enjoyment from showing off and though I try conscientiously to suppress this, and though when a lack of suppression frequently backfires uncomfortably, I continue to become at times the "smart aleck" that in the years of discipline from my parents used to get me sent to my room. This time it got me sent to the galley. Mr. Walley was far too self-effacing and considerate of others to have suggested a morning refreshment but I had to flaunt my knowledge of English customs by asking if he would care for his "elevenses." Of course he accepted my suggestion and knowledge. Sophy, who by reason of over thirty years of friendship knows me uncomfortably well, grinned wickedly as she said, "Wasn't that clever of you to know about elevenses? You don't mind fixing it?"

As I edged around her and Mr. Walley toward the door to the cabin, I realized for the first time what I had taken to be part of the machinery of the *Venturer* was a motorcycle propped against the far side of the space we were in. Our departure had been so enveloped by the confusion and surprise of a group to see us off, a turn-around under a shed, and then a lock, I had given no attention to what was immediately around us. I had had, however, a fleeting impression, as I was helped into the boat, the space in the stern seemed less than when we had explored it the day before. Certainly I had not realized this was due to the presence of a motorcycle since that was one of the last

44

objects I could have conceived of including in nautical equipment. Even now I thought it probable my ignorance of any sort of machine might have prompted me to make a false identification; therefore I inquired of Mr. Walley

as I pointed, "Could that be a motorcycle?" Mr. Walley leaned over from the tiller to pat it with affectionate pride, and Sophy bent forward to look around him at the object, her eyes widening so I realized she had not previously been aware of it. "I brought it along," Mr. Walley told

us, "so I could get home in the evening." I know Sophy's
jaw dropped; I think mine did. "Home?" she echoed
faintly. Mr. Walley nodded serenely. "For the first three
nights that is. After that I'll sleep on the boat, but until
then we won't have got so far I can't get back easily."

CHAPTER FOUR

A LITTLE later in the morning we tied up and went ashore at Mr. Walley's suggestion. There was a place nearby he thought we would like to see. In canal cruising a dock is not necessary for landing. One giant step bridges the distance from ship to shore, so a pause is accomplished as easily as stopping a car by the side of the road. With Mr. Walley in the lead we followed the towpath a few yards in the direction from which we had come, going around a bridge under which we had recently passed. He took us across a field to a road, along that a short distance, and onto a stone bridge over a wide, shallow stream. A family was picnicking on its bank, the children clambering over large rocks that jutted above the water. We were looking at the river Trent, Mr. Walley told us, but actually what Sophy and I were looking at with puzzled interest was the bridge itself. A long span, perhaps six feet wide, was interrupted on either side at regular intervals by a series of pointed niches like the teeth of a saw. Mr. Walley assured us he'd been told the pattern was not rare in England. The reason for such indentation was that any pedestrian who might have the ill luck to be on the bridge at the moment the hunt crossed over, might wedge himself into one of these crevices. Conceding this a mark of consideration, I would still count it something less than a happy spot from which to view a pack of hounds and a clutch of spirited horses.

Mr. Walley indicated the driveway on the far side of the bridge. This would take us to the house itself, he said, Shugborough Hall, the seat of the Earl of Lichfield. He would wait for us at the boat.

There are woods on either side of the river. They make the water dark and shadowed but when the driveway has passed the last line of trees it opens to a meadow on that Sunday solidly overlaid with buttercups. Curving to the right, the driveway continues between two rows of rhododendron nearly twenty feet high, I think. Sophy had with her the pamphlet *Historic Houses and Castles,* and we found in it that Shugborough is open every Sunday from 2 to 6 from May 26th to September 29th. We did not go nearer the house however. We did not want to linger until two o'clock, and the meadow, we said, would be full compensation.

On our way back to the *Venturer* Sophy feasted on another spectacle that very nearly took her off the bank. We were on the towpath when she clutched my arm. "Look at that," she ordered in a hoarse whisper, "young love in the hedgerows. Just like English novels." I corroborated her discovery with considerable interest but nothing like the intensive, rapturous scrutiny of Sophy. This caused her to put one foot in front of the other in dreamy abstraction, drawn by the magnet of the two lovers across the way. She realized where her wandering step had led her only

48

when one failed to find solid ground beneath. She very nearly walked into the canal and what saved her was as animated a piece of choreography as I have witnessed in any ballet. Arms revolving fast as a child's windmill in a breeze, unattached limb elevated until she was very nearly riven, she leaned back in an arch that would have been commendable in a young dancer but at her age was spectacular. After a moment of spellbound wonder I hurried forward and fulfilled the function of sustaining partner in a *pas de deux*, although not in the traditional pose. I clutched the soloist by the seat of her slacks and pulled. She regained the ground she had lost and we continued on our way with no words but considerable breathiness from the recent performer. The young lovers had not been in any way distracted.

We sat on the bank to eat the lunch I had prepared while Sophy was testing her muscles for possible sprains. We ate crusty fresh bread, spread with rich butter, country ham and a bowl of lettuce. By the grace of the Crown Hotel and my persuasiveness we had ice from the yellow plastic bucket in my tea in a tall glass. Mr. Walley said he had heard of people doing such a thing to a cup of tea but this was the first he had seen. He declined my offer to share it.

We had not been long on our way again when we came into the midst of sportive activity. Along this stretch the Shropshire Union Canal is as wide as the Thames. It was startling to emerge from the narrow channel in which there had been no boat other than ours into water peppered by small craft of almost every description—canoes, kayaks, even little sailboats—peopled by fathers with children, sometimes entire families including the dog. We moved even more slowly than our normal speed through this kaleidoscope, but within a few minutes the canal narrowed again and we were alone on a narrow strip of water, laid flat like a strip of carpeting on the meadows.

I was washing the dishes when we came to the next lock. Humming with contentment, sniffing with pleasure the heavy blend of country smells the breeze was bringing in through the open window, I could not know my hands and feet were being set in a mold that would not vary in the days and weeks ahead, I at the sink, a lock or a bridge ahead.

Mr. Walley called from the stern, "Would you close the windows, please, and, Mrs. Jacobs, could I have your help? Both the gates are closed." A very curious thing occurs I find whenever Sophy and I travel together. After only a brief acquaintanceship with both of us, anyone requiring competent physical assistance invariably and instantly selects Sophy.

I had difficulty with the windows. They were hinged across the top and opened out, held in place by a metal bar with holes at intervals along it. One of these holes, according to how much air was wanted, had to be fitted over a tiny knob on the sill and consequently released to bring the window back into place. A sense of urgency made me fumble but I had no help from Sophy. The first call from Mr. Walley reached her sunning in the bow and she had loped past me eager as a beagle at the call of a huntsman's horn. When I had finished my task and sealed us in she was at the tiller. I saw only her feet and legs through the open door of the cabin. When I reached the stern I found she was standing on the bench there in order, she said, to see over the roof. Mr. Walley was ashore, windlass hanging down the back of his neck. When he had opened the first gates he went ahead at a half run toward the farther pair calling Sophy to bring the boat along. Sophy put the engine into gear—Mr. Walley must have shown her how to do this while I was closing the windows—and then put her hands to the tiller and pushed with what I could see was all her might. Almost immediately the nose of the boat butted the side wall of the lock and jarred us. Sophy pulled back the tiller hard. "Damn," she said, and put us against the other wall. Mr. Walley called back, "Don't fret, you'll have it soon. Easy does it. Now hold her back from the gates."

Exertion and mortification had reddened Sophy's face. "The bow is so far off," she said and was panting a little. "And the breeze shifted." A sailor would not have called this delicious zephyr a stiff breeze. It was enough, however, I realized, to affect a long boat. I watched her next maneuver with unqualified admiration. I would not have had the slightest notion of how or when to slow the engine, reverse when we came almost within touch of the lock and then repeat the sequence. We churned the water considerably as we advanced and retreated but we did not buck a wall again nor the gate. When Mr. Walley jumped aboard again he said Sophy had done a fine job and he was glad of two at the locks. The red of Sophy's face turned a shade deeper.

Something wet on my cheek startled me and as I brushed it away I looked for the source of moisture on a sunny day in calm water. We were gliding through clouds of foam billowing around us to such a height that flecks from it had

52

reached my cheek. I pointed at it too astonished to speak.

"It's detergent," Mr. Walley explained. "The folk that live along the canal empty the water from their washing into it. It gets stored up in the pound and when a boat goes through that churns it up and makes the foam." I had not known just what to expect on this trip but certainly one thing I had not anticipated I said with conviction was a boat in a bubble bath.

"Sometimes," Mr. Walley said, "it can come clean up over the side."

Sophy and I went to the bow and sat on its rail, one on either side. There was not room for chairs but after a few moments we brought out cushions that made the sitting easier. I had with me a book about the canals but it was hard to focus on a page when there was so much to see: sheep in the meadows, and cows that at our approach came hurrying down to the edge of the water. Arriving there, they behaved like spectators at a tennis match. Simultaneously as we passed they moved their heads to watch us.

Moorhens with shiny black bodies and crimson beaks swam ahead of us in agitation, and reaching a bank scurried among the reeds. On the shore they bobbed their heads continuously as I have seen old people do, talking to themselves. Frequently we caught up with or met coming toward us a family of swans. Sometimes the parents were outraged at the encounter and the father prepared to make an issue of it. While the mother gathered close around her the cygnets and headed them toward shore turning her back on our boat in order to conceal her brood, the father came at us. Neck out, wings spread as though he were hunching his shoulders and every feather on them separate and erect, he would advance. One even more irascible than the others took off from the water and came at us. Fortunately he came down again directly beneath our bow because Sophy and I with an identical purpose in mind were wedged together in the doorway to the cabin.

We heard a cuckoo. I had heard only one other in my life and that had been calling from an olive grove at Delphi in Greece. To hear it a second time on a yellow afternoon in Shropshire made the landscape misty before my silly sentimental eyes. It was impossible to communicate with Mr. Walley standing over the engine and in that noise I thought he had not heard the bird. But when I reached him on the run, to call his attention to the sound, he was leaning far out over the side of the boat, one hand on the tiller, the other cupped behind his ear. "Aye," he said, "I'm hearing him, and looking for a bare tree. That's where you'll see him. Cuckoo always calls from a leafless tree." "We have a naturalist with us," I repeated to Sophy.

The booklet I was endeavoring to read is called *Know*

Your Waterways by Robert Aickman. Putting my attention to it, I learned the inland waterways system dates from 1761 when the third Duke of Bridgewater opened the Bridgewater Canal in Lancashire. The purpose of the canal was to carry coal from his mines at Worsley to Manchester but there is some ambiguity about the actual reason for its construction. The book says the motivation was the unhappy circumstance that his grace was crossed in love in London causing him to retire to his Lancashire estate. Why a flouting should turn his thoughts to carrying coal, I cannot say. Nevertheless, once his attention was diverted the Duke employed a millwright named James Brindley so wanting in education he could scarcely sign his name; yet he planned the entire canal system and was its engineer as well. Brindley waterways are called "contour canals" because they follow the rise and fall and curves of the terrain.

There are only two systems, Brindley and Telford. Thomas Telford was a Scotsman. His method of construction was to cut straight through to a given point, using a series of locks to achieve mountain levels and descents on the other side. Within fifty or sixty years of the opening in 1761 nearly four thousand miles of waterways were constructed and until the railways came these were the cause of England's quick rise to industrial prosperity. The appearance of the railways, however, marked the beginning of a decline in the use of the canals for commercial transportation. More recently the invasion on the highways of transportation trucks has threatened the very survival of these water lanes. Therefore, the Inland Waterways Association was formed in 1946 for the purpose of keeping navigable the canals, urging their use for commerce and promoting their desirability for pleasure travel.

Sophy interrupted my reading with the suggestion Mr. Walley might like his tea, adding she would join him in the stern in case he needed her assistance. I had not needed her reminder to know my place and hers, but I did not begrudge her the position outside. I had no envy to be involved with that tiller and engine. However, I did find the inside stuffy because I had forgotten to open the windows again when we had left the lock. I put the kettle on and then began the job of opening the windows along one side and back the other. I had just fitted the last metal brace into place and the kettle was simmering on the threshold of a full boil when Mr. Walley called, "Lock ahead. Would you shut the windows please?" Back I went down one line and up the other lifting and pulling the metal braces. Then I turned the stove off and emptied the contents of the kettle into a pan so that I could use the hot water for washing up the tea things. I regretted audibly, though no one could hear me, I had ever read English novels with all the talk in them about tea having to be made with freshly boiled water and certainly not allowed to stand. I had an ominous feeling as I muttered at my work this was how it was going to be throughout the trip! Windows, tea and a lock. My crystal-gazing turned out to be right in all but one prognostication. I could have made the tea and let it brew until it matched lye in strength, but was so reduced in temperature it was something less than tepid. I only discovered this at the end of a week, when my witless timing brought us to a lock as usual just after I had made the tea. At a hail from Sophy and Mr. Walley I had set it down in a flurry of pleasure at being asked to help in their superior work. I had discovered they wanted me to leap to the bank with a coil of rope in my hands, and having left them in no doubt that nothing on earth would induce me to hazard any such preposterously broad jump, I had returned to the cabin leaving them to work out the problem for themselves. Inside, brooding over my incompetence and the indignity of its having been tested, I had forgotten the tea but later when I had admitted this oversight and apologized to Mr. Walley for making him wait until I had brewed a fresh batch, he had urged me with decidedly more eagerness than he had heretofore shown to bring it to him as it was. Drinking his second cup he had said this had body to it and that I was a fine teamaker; he had been concerned, he said, that a shopkeeper had sold a poor brand with no taste to it, but had not wanted to mention it after all the trouble I was taking. I realized at that moment what I had been serving him before had been in his opinion scarcely an eyewash. What he was drinking had so much body there was scarcely need of a cup around it.

CHAPTER FIVE

THE lock we reached at teatime was Park Gate and we were held up there for an hour and a half. I had thought as I rushed from window to window either I was getting quicker at my tasks or it was taking an unconscionable time to start the elevator ride. In the early part of the day we had been on a down slope of the land; now we were climbing and I knew at this lock we would be raised to the level of the channel beyond. But when I went to the stern to find out what was going on I discovered we had not yet gone into the pound. We weren't going up or anywhere Sophy explained because there was not enough water coming in to open the gates. Mr. Walley had gone ahead to find out the cause. Before he left he had told her we had been traveling over very shallow water. Careful maneuvering was required to keep our craft in the channel and not run aground.

I reminded Sophy we had both heard Mr. Lloyd at Stone assuring Mr. Walley that word from along the line was the water was coming in and we were to have no difficulty. Mr. Walley had accepted this assurance with some reservation I thought. Sophy had asked him about this, she told me, while they were working together and I was, of course, below, and Mr. Walley had explained there had been considerable work done over the preceding weeks in the locks and along some of the banks. This had necessitated draining out the water. The work had been completed at the time promised but when the engineers had commenced the program of refilling the drained areas they had discovered the drought that had prevailed in England over many weeks had so reduced the streams scarcely any supply was coming from them. Sophy had also learned Mr. Walley was ordinarily a construction man on the maintenance crew but had been released from that in order to take us on our cruise. "That's why," she said, "he was dubious about Mr. Lloyd's guarantee of plenty of water. Mr. Walley's the one who really knows."

I made tea for Sophy and me and as we were drinking it storm clouds came over the sky and the air became chilly. We went inside to get sweaters and decided this was a good time to sort out and put away the supplies and our clothes. When we had finished this and returned outside there was still no sign of Mr. Walley, but a boy riding along the tow-path on a bicycle paused at our hail and gave us news. There was a boat ahead he said that had gone aground. "The party aboard," he explained in an accent so rich with Shropshire flavor as to be almost unintelligible to us, "have been trying to float her by letting water in from the lock. Amachoors," he added shaking his head. "They've mucked it up proper." He pushed the ground impatiently with one foot and rode off. Sophy shuddered a little. "But for the grace of God," she said, "the 'amachoors' could be you and me."

"I wish I thought you'd remember that the next time we travel," was my answer. "But just like Ed Murrow's program, I can see and hear it now. 'Why do we want a guide or a driver or a captain or whatever? *I* can do it.' "

"Would you care for a drink?" Sophy inquired and went inside.

We were in the main cabin when Mr. Walley returned. Sophy had just taken from a shoebag a bottle of Scotch for herself, a bottle of white wine for me and soda to be shared.

In addition to the title of executive Sophy holds on every trip the office of wine steward. However assorted the tastes of her traveling companions may be, she supplies the favored choice. The receptacle for this list is always a shoebag. She eyes with disfavor a carrier designed to hold bottles of liquor, though these are obtainable in any luggage shop and include such convenient accessories as glasses, a cocktail shaker and other oddments. Sophy refuses this accommodation because she says it is not only ostentatious but too purposeful. Such inconvenience as is incurred by having to remove several pairs of shoes before the liquor can be got at is outweighed by the spirit of casualness this evokes. It is not a logical motivation, but it is Philadelphian.

Mr. Walley brought news the water was being let out of the lock above so that the pound below, where the boat was stuck, would be filling. We could move ahead, and with a rope from our boat help float the stranded group. We put away the bottles and the shoebag. A pattern was already taking shape that no matter how leisurely cruising on a canal may be, how many hours go by without any activity required, the instant a specific action is undertaken such as a meal, a drink or reading a book, a thunderclap of emergency shatters the project.

We found the stranded "amachoors" a mile and a half from the spot at which we had been moored. Mr. Walley had walked there, investigated the situation, given advice, promised help, and then walked back. No wonder, Sophy said, we had been waiting a considerable time, but even more wonder a man should do that stint with no effort and no more mention of it than one of us might have called attention to a walk to the corner drugstore.

The boat aground was a cabin cruiser not a converted barge like ours. It had not so flat a bottom and it drew more water. This was why it had gone aground. Its navigator had not erred from the center channel and for this very reason we could not pass and perhaps this was just as well because under the circumstances I did not care to ask myself how good a Samaritan I would have been. The circumstances were dismal. Over the last hour the temperature had dropped and brought down with it a thin dispiriting rain; not full-bodied drops of a quick, energetic shower, but an anemic, nagging drizzle.

Mr. Walley eased the *Venturer* as close to the bank as he dared, relinquished the tiller to Sophy and made a spectacular jump to the bank. His instructions were to return the *Venturer* to midchannel and hold her there. We scraped a little in the passage but did not stick. Sophy kept the engine idling in order not to drift and held us in place. I brought a raincoat for each of us from the back of the cupboard where we had optimistically hung them.

A sizable group of people was assembled on the towpath. Perhaps the number seemed large to me because the sum of all the people we had seen during the day would not have equaled this. From the range of age and unequal distribution of sex I felt it unlikely they had all of them been in the hedgerows like the couple Sophy and I had seen at noon. They must have come from a village and that gave me the idea Sophy and I could abandon the ship and go to the local pub for warmth and perhaps an added solace of a beer.

"Are we near a village?" I called to Mr. Walley. "Aye," he answered, "Penkridge. We're havin' a good rain now," he added with satisfaction. He leaned toward us and spoke in a lower tone. "Folk like to take an evening stroll along the towpath. They'll help us wi' a poosh."

Sophy knew it had been in my mind to leave the boat and walk to the village. "Care for a stroll?" she asked.

I dropped the idea, pulled the hood of my raincoat further over my head and went through the cabins to watch the rescue from the bow. I knew if I stayed with her one of us would suggest, and I knew it would be I, we count this day's run a canal trip and go back to London or even New York. I had had enough of cold and rain and witless people strolling in it, and a passageway so narrow you couldn't pass anyone in trouble and had to stop to help whether you wanted to or not, and I did not want. Sophy might agree with me and if she did she would immediately start a correspondence that would not only cancel this trip but the succeeding one including the Lindsays and Arthur Kober, get a return passage and the next thing I knew I would be walking into my apartment in New York closed for the summer and the cook on vacation

62

in Vermont. I settled myself in the bow of the *Venturer*.

None of the strollers helped with a "poosh" but they separately and in chorus offered considerable advice, all unintelligible to me although I could hear the syllables clearly. Mr. Walley, I think, followed none of it although he responded frequently and courteously with "Aye, that's right. Aye, that's right." The occupants of the cruiser were sitting on the roof of their boat. They were five men, very young and not appealing, so there was nothing inviting nor rewarding about helping them except our own release. They were shoving one another about in a horseplay of pretending to trip up and send a victim overboard and they were all giggling. Their faces, shirts, slacks and sneakers were dirty. When Mr. Walley called from the bank, however, they stopped jostling about and gave him immediate attention. He told three of them to jump ashore and they did promptly and unsuccessfully. Each one landed in the water at the foot of the bank and came up to the top muddy now as well as dirty. The strollers had extended helping hands and considerable laughter and the boys good-humoredly joined them, maintaining the level of humor by shaking their trouser legs free of water and mud at the spectators nearest them.

Mr. Walley threw one end of the rope he carried to two boys on the cruiser, who were standing in the bow. He told them to make it fast. One of them did this while another at Mr. Walley's instruction uncoiled their own mooring rope and threw one end over to Mr. Walley, who gave it to the three passengers ashore and told them to pull when he gave the word. He called to the two on board, "Now rock your boat when I say. One of you stand on

63

either side." They separated, taking the positions he indicated. There was no deck around the cruiser but on either side there was a narrow ledge barely wide enough to walk along in Indian fashion. Each boy stood on this amidships facing the other and bending over the roof, holding on to a cleat fastened there. When Mr. Walley called, "Rock," they seesawed the boat from side to side. At the same time Mr. Walley pulled on the rope he held, moving forward or trying to as he did this. He carried the rope over his shoulder holding it with both hands in front of him. He bent forward pulling with such strength and force his head was bowed below his knees. At rhythmic intervals in a voice with neither tremor nor breathlessness he called, "Rock, rock, rock." The three of the crew on shore waited with their rope and his instructions. He would tell them, he said, when he was ready. As Mr. Walley strained, pulled and called, the crowd quieted into watchful silence. Presently all of us heard a faint scratching sound no more than the noise a cat makes who wants to be let into the house; but this was the sound of the boat moving a little. When we heard it a second time Mr. Walley called, "Now, boys, pull toward you but not hard," and to those on the boat, "Keep rocking." Almost immediately he changed his orders to the boys on the rope. "Forward now," he said, "after me." In the silence after these commands we heard another scrape, then no more sound. The boat was moving and Mr. Walley's back began to straighten. We could all of us see the strain easing until presently his head was up, he was erect, marching not plowing into the ground, drawing the motor cruiser behind him with no more effort than a little boy requires to draw his express wagon. The boys on the

64

boat stopped rocking it and moved forward to sit in the bow, dangling their legs over the side and wiping the sweat from their foreheads. They were breathing heavily. The three boys on shore caught up with Mr. Walley and each took hold of the rope behind him though there was no need of their assistance now. He led the way to a widening in the channel, sent the three boys back to the stern telling them to pull gently toward them and did the same with his bow rope. This was the way they eased the cruiser out of the main channel, over to the side so that we might pass.

When Mr. Walley came back to us I asked if the boys had thanked him. "Oh aye," he said. "They're nice lads. Just a bit careless with their fooling about." When we passed their boat a few minutes later the boys were inside. We could see them through the windows of their cabin. They must have heard our engine and known there was no other boat in the vicinity but no one came to the window to wave and if they thanked Mr. Walley once they did not overdo it by a repetition.

We tied up at Penkridge at a quarter to eight. "The proper village," Mr. Walley said, "is just up the road a bit." Had the bit been only a hundred yards I would not have walked it, tired as I was and long as the day had been. We had counted on making purchases for our supper but the shops would be closed by now. We would have to eat dinner at the local inn. Sophy asked where the inn was. "Not far, I hope," she added. Hunger had evidently put us on the same train of thought. Mr. Walley said he did not know of an inn round about that could put people up for the night but there was a pub just across the way. "You follow this towpath," he said pointing to the one along which we were moored. "It will take you up to the main road. It's only a step and directly across on the other side of the road is a pub. You must mind the road," he cautioned. "It's a highway and the cars come along the bend there at a shocking speed." Mr. Walley was pulling his motorcycle from the place in the stern where he had wedged it and I murmured to Sophy I took it very kindly at my age to have someone express a fatherly apprehension about my crossing a road safely.

A man in working clothes came along the towpath on a bicycle. Mr. Walley hailed him to ask a hand in getting his own vehicle off the boat. We asked our captain if he would not prefer to stay aboard considering the day he had had both in length and in work but he said he was not tired, his wife would worry if he were not there and that it was only about an hour's run to Newport Salop (Shropshire) where he lived. About the same distance, he explained, as it was from Stone.

"About the same length of time in today's run," Sophy murmured "that it took me to fly from New York to London."

The two men lifted the motorcycle over the side of the *Venturer* and to the towpath. The workman rode away on his bicycle. Mr. Walley stamped on the pedal to start the machine, jumped on and rode off after the bicycle. It was very still when he had gone, no boat but ours within sight on the canal. On the far side of the towpath beside us there was a row of little cottages but each one was dark. No one came walking our way. Once more Sophy brought out the shoebag and this time nothing interrupted us. We were in no hurry, we decided, to have dinner. We would be glad

66

just to sit down for a little while, have a drink in leisure and then a nice hot dinner across the way.

The pub was crowded with noisy men when we reached it about an hour later. We did not see any women in the room and standing in the doorway we received such astonished attention we backed out simultaneously and in considerable haste. After a consultation on the path we decided to try the back entrance. Perhaps the dining room was in that section of the building. Again I knew my place. If there is any verbal inquiring to be made I must be the spokesman.

The back door was open. We looked into a large kitchen with low wooden beams across the ceiling, and a heavy brass lamp swinging over a long rough wood table. Seated around this were several men and two women. They were eating, and the smell of the food was delicious. I stepped across the threshold, Sophy hanging back of course. "Good evening," I said. "May we have some dinner?"

Once when I was a child I invited myself to dinner at the house of a friend. The request was received kindly there but when permission was asked of my mother over the telephone and she sensed by what means the invitation had come about, I was ordered to come home immediately. Subsequent activity on her part removed my inclination to involve myself in society by that method ever again.

It was obvious the moment I made my request at the inn that in spite of the years between I had repeated myself. The diners put down their implements, looked at one another, at me, and not a word was spoken for as long a time as it took me to wish myself far, far away from there, preferably as far as Muncie, Indiana, where I might start over.

Finally one of the women spoke. "We've got nothing here but what we're eating ourselves," she said. From the heat of my face I must have blushed to a magenta temperature. "I beg your pardon," I said, "I was told you served meals here."

"Well, we don't," the woman answered. "This is a pub and there is nothing but drinks served out front in the bar." I do not know why I became suddenly angry unless it was because I was cold and tired and hungry and looking at other people eating hot food not offering me any, and in addition making me feel I had made a fool of myself. Knowing I had done just that I spoke sharply.

"I'm sorry. I misunderstood," I said, "but we do need food. A friend and I are cruising on the canal. We were held up at Park Gate lock and we only got in a short time ago. If you don't serve food, have you any supplies I could buy from you that we could cook on the boat?" The woman got up from the table and came toward me and suddenly she seemed a different person. "Now I'm sorry," she said, "that's surely too bad. I'll tell you what I can do. I've got some eggs I brought in not an hour ago fresh laid from my own hens. You're welcome to buy those and I can spare you some butter. You could make yourself a nice dish of eggs and I may have a little bit of bacon put by I could spare." Dinner at Claridge's would not have appealed to me so much at that moment as this exquisite dish of eggs with a little bit of bacon put by. My mouth so filled with moisture I could scarcely thank her articulately.

She brought the provisions to me in a little basket that I promised to return next morning and I paid her. When I left, not another person at the table had spoken a word since my arrival, nor had Sophy come nearer to the threshold than the ten-foot distance at which she had stopped on our arrival. I gave her the news and indicated our provisions. She was as happy as I in the change of plan, agreeing it would be much pleasanter to eat in our own house than in the noisy, smoky place I had quitted even had meals been provided there. As we returned along the towpath we saw lights in the upper stories of the little houses that fringed it. "The families have been out for a stroll on the towpath," Sophy observed. "Now they are going to bed."

In our own house we drew the chintz curtains across the windows and turned on our lights. Evenings are long in England in the spring and summer, but this evening at ten o'clock, it had been gray since midafternoon when the rain had started. It was still drizzling in a petulant half-hearted way that dampened and chilled the surroundings. We had been told to be chary of using the electric lights lest we run down the battery that also fed the starter of our engine. I promised it would only take a few minutes to cook our succulent meal and we would go immediately after to bed. "We're like those people in the houses," I pointed out, "going to bed early to save electricity, except that I'm thoroughly done in and I've taken no stroll."

Sophy lowered the table from the wall and took from the shelves and drawers china, glass, silver and linen. "I call this utter heaven," she said.

I went to the stern, lifted the lid of the bench there and revolved the cap that turned on the gas as I had done during the day. Mr. Walley had said it was not necessary to shut off the gas at the tank each time I finished using the stove but we must be sure to turn it off at night lest there be a small leak and that could be dangerous when we were closed in and asleep. I had thought it better to establish the habit at the beginning of turning it off each time so there would be no possibility of forgetting it at night. I left the top of the bench open since I would return to give it the final turning off for the night but I closed the door to the stern cabin to keep out the dampness and the chill.

"Once I've started cooking," I told Sophy, "the heat of the stove will warm up this room. I'll make an omelet," I announced, "not just scrambled eggs." I broke the eggs into a bowl, beat them up, added a tablespoon of cold water for each egg, put a piece of butter in the heavy skillet, set it on the stove and turning on the gas applied a match. Nothing whatever happened.

"Oh drat," I said, "I didn't turn it on enough at the tank."

Sophy looked up from setting the table. "We don't have to be that economical," she advised. "Give it the works. I'm really cold."

I went back to the stern, unlocking and opening the end cabin door. This time I turned the tap as far as it would go and retraced my path, closing the cabin door behind me. "This will do it," I prophesied and applied a match. I held the match over the ring until it had burned my fingers. Still holding the charred stick in my hand I backed to the bunk and sat down on it. "Sophy," I said, "there's something the matter with the gas tank. Not one particle of gas is coming through."

Sophy didn't believe me. She was better at mechanics,

she said, than I. I'd probably turned it the wrong way or something. I come from a family of engineers and my father and grandfather taught me left and right by demonstrating that a valve opening is to the right and a valve closing is to the left. However, I felt this was not the moment to bring up the matter of my education. I felt, too, if Sophy could bring gas to the stove by any means I would certainly not hold for principles, nor even call to her attention the fact that I was the one who had been turning the gas on and off all day. Presently she returned. "Now try it," she said. I did and burned my fingers the second time with a match; the stove was as unresponsive as before. Sophy and I looked at each other. "There is no gas," I said, and this was probably as unnecessary an observation as anyone has ever made.

I went to the stern once more, shut off the valve, replaced the top of the bench, closed and locked the door of the end cabin and found Sophy taking from the breadbox on the shelf under the sink a thin end of the loaf from which during the day I had cut the sturdy thick slices Mr. Walley favored. We divided the delicate remnant between us and spread it with some of the butter we had bought from the pub, nibbling it slowly to make it last. Sophy peeked through our curtains. "They're all in bed now," she said. "Not a light showing. We can't ask them for any help."

We did not talk any more as we undressed, other than a few words exchanged over drawing lots for cabins, and a deplorable phrase from me at the sight of my flat hot-water bottle on my bed ready to be filled. Sophy drew the center cabin and I the stern. We had already agreed to leave the forecabin for Mr. Walley's occupancy when he settled in.

I put on my bathrobe over my nightgown, wondering at the time with shivering bitterness what had possessed me to bring along nylon. If I remained on this trip, though I thought that highly unlikely; I would provide myself with something neat in flannel—high neck and long sleeves. I took a sweater into bed with me and once under the covers wrapped it around my feet. I had a box of Kleenex beside me because I had not entirely recovered from the cold that had put me to bed at Madame Pandit's. Sophy called "Good night." I answered her with no additional comment. We switched off our lights almost simultaneously. Probably, like me, she was too dispirited to read or possibly afraid the electricity would expire like the gas. I did not ask her; I was thinking about Madame Pandit's house, the beautiful big bedroom there, the lovely wide, soft bed in which I had had such a happy, luxurious cold; and I was asking myself why I should have left it voluntarily to lay myself on the equivalent of an ironing board under a mound of covering scarcely softer or more pliable than layers of sheet metal!

CHAPTER SIX

SOPHY and I were awake and up at six though each of us admitted, a little testily on my part, she had slept soundly. I had wanted to brood over my misery and plan the things I would say about the kind of treat it was to cruise on a canal, and make out a list of the people to whom I would say this. But in the very middle of a phrase acid enough to blister I had dropped off and had not awakened until light through the curtains roused me. Furthermore it was sunlight and that is not an inducement to brooding or acid prose. It brought me to my feet instead. I was still hungry but I admitted ruefully to myself, as I pulled back the curtains, nothing would induce me to give up this trip. The water twinkled in the sunlight. On the side of the canal away from us a meadow of buttercups and grass washed by the rain had a shining face. From my window I saw a workman riding a bicycle along the towpath, whistling, a lunchbox on a strap over his shoulder. I left the window and began to dress, hurrying because I wanted to be out in the sunshine and also I wanted food. Sophy called from her cabin, "Look out your window on the far side." I returned to the post I had recently left in time to see a rather corpulent, elderly gentleman in the toils of two Sealyhams. The dogs were in high spirit and on the end of long leather leads. The length was achieved, I could see, by hooking together and then attaching to the collar of each, three average-sized leashes. This ingenuity was evidently designed to give the dogs

greater freedom and wider radius of movement on the walk without allowing them to run free so close to the canal and highway. The pets were enjoying their freedom but reducing the radius considerably by running round and round the gentleman. He in turn was endeavoring to break this circuit though, hobbled as he was by the leashes, his own activity was curtailed. He carried a walking stick and this he was waving about in the air, shouting at the same time, "Now then, sir. Stop that. Stop that, I say. Enough. Enough. What are you trying to do?"

Who could say what they were trying to do, but with rapture I could see what they succeeded in doing. With one final whirl around, chasing each other, they bound their leader in a final lasso that caught him up completely and deposited him in a sitdown on the towpath. His hat of hairy wool or felt, bright green with a cockade on the side, was jolted over his eyes almost down to his mustaches that quivered tremulously beneath. His shouts stopped abruptly as he thumped to a seat. The dogs left off circling immediately he was on an accessible level. One on either side, forepaws on each of his shoulders, they licked his face, pushing the hat up a little. The gentleman, and if he had not at one time been an army colonel then all the cartoon caricatures have lied, had dropped his stick in the fall. With his two hands he alternately endeavored to push the dogs away and unwrap the leashes from around his legs as though he were unwinding the puttees he may have worn in the First World War. When he bent over in the process of extricating himself the dogs transferred their affection to the back of his neck. When he straightened up to push them off they sprang for the leashes, worrying them with the make-believe of having a bone in their jaws. Voice had returned to their victim but not articulate speech. He injected into the early-morning air hoarse bellows with no syllabic content. In the end he won, and moved off down the path limping a little. On the back of his hat there was a fragment of torn brim that hung on a slender thread, chewed on evidently but not entirely bitten off. Watching him out of sight I knew my day could not have had a better start and I sang a little tune as I finished dressing.

By consultation Sophy and I decided we must not both of us be so far and so long away that news of the gas failure would not be given Mr. Walley as soon as he arrived. The amount we would purchase in the village to forestall the repetition of last night's bare cupboard would require two carriers. Therefore, we would not set out on that excursion until after Mr. Walley's arrival. Sophy volunteered to try the pub again for something hot if only water for tea. That she should have volunteered to make vocal inquiry made me realize hunger had sapped her resistance. She was gone long enough for me to make both beds and do an over-all sweeping and dusting. When she came she was on the run.

"The pub was closed," she said panting a little. "Tight shut, front and back, but the woman in the next cottage is going to give us water for our tea." She snatched up our kettle as she spoke and hurried away again, calling back to me, "Come and see, come and see." I left my broom and dust pan and followed her along the towpath toward the highway. A few yards beyond our boat, between it and the road where the canal rounding a curve left a triangular plot of ground, was a tiny cottage and a garden behind it, all enclosed by a white fence. I had scarcely been aware of it on our way to and from the pub in the rainy dusk of the evening before but in the bright sun and early-morning freshness I could not have hurried by. In shape and relative size it might have been a model for gingerbread houses that confectioners sell at Christmas time, except that this was white. Even the flowers blooming there were small and circumspect although lavish in color and profusion. The open casement windows were tiny, and so was the chimney above them. Perhaps this was why the smoke curling out of it was thin and delicate.

A woman was taking the kettle from Sophy's hand as I reached them at the fence. She was explaining to Sophy with apology, and an accent thick and rich as cream, she would put our kettle on at once. She paused to smile at me and say good morning. She was young, slender, with brown skin and pink cheeks like Mr. Walley's. She had dark eyes like his too but considerably more hair, parted in the middle and drawn smooth into a knot at the back. Her teeth were very white. She was not pretty but lively and warm. She continued her explanation as she led us to the house urging us to come in and apologizing again that we must wait a few minutes. My height is about five foot five, I think, perhaps a very little more, but I had to duck my head as I went through the doorway. The room on the other side was low ceilinged and beamed overhead. There were casement windows on two sides, open, the sunlight a smoky shaft slicing the room diagonally. There was a little smoke from the fireplace, but only enough to carry into the room a delicious blend of wood burning and bacon. The fireplace covered one wall of the room and breakfast was cooking on it. I had never before seen a meal actually prepared over an open indoor fire and I do not remember seeing anything that appealed to me more than this sight. Bacon in a pan was sizzling on a ledge a few inches above the hearth and well into the recess of the fireplace proper; the handle protruded toward the room so the pan could be easily removed when the dish was done. A brass kettle

77

on a crane now swung in toward the fire was starting to boil, clouds of steam coming in puffs from its spout. In front of the fireplace a little way back from the hearth was a table with three chairs drawn up to it, on it a spotless blue-and-white-checked cloth. The china was white with a flower pattern. Our hostess had sent us into the house. She came in carrying our kettle filled now with water from the pump at the back of her garden. She removed the brass kettle from the hob and replaced it with ours. "I'm very sorry," she said, "I'm afraid it's going to blacken your kettle." Any evidence of heat inside and out of that kettle was so welcome a sight we found it difficult to say moderately how little we minded the blacking. The delay in putting on our kettle she explained was because she must let her own boil first since her husband and son must have their breakfast and be off to work and to school without delay. Their tea and porridge must be ready when they came to the table. Porridge then I knew was in a pot that swung over the fire on a crane of its own. While we waited for our kettle to boil we told her about our trip. I doubt that Martians will evoke greater surprise when they visit us than we saw in the eyes of that young woman of Penkridge. "Fancy that," she said over and over again. Evidently making a swift calculation of relative distances in her mind she added, "Someday I may go to London myself."

When our kettle began to shake and send out noises of an approaching boil she looked from one to the other of us and asked for our teapot. "Oh," Sophy said, "I didn't bother to bring that. We'll just take the kettle back to the boat." Our benefactor stood transfixed. "You've not brought the pot?" she asked. "Why then you must go and

78

get it quickly." This time I demurred. I thought if I waited much longer for a cup of hot tea I might forget to a high-pitched degree my British watchword of "restraint." Therefore, with controlled firmness I repeated we would take the kettle with us to the boat.

Reluctantly and shaking her head in evident bewildered disapproval she took our kettle from the hob and relinquished it to us. Again we thanked her and hurried off. At the little gate from the garden I turned back. She was standing stooped in the doorway watching us. I waved and she waved back but halfheartedly. However, she smiled then and wished us a good trip, saying she was glad to have made our acquaintance.

All in a tremor of haste I put the kettle down on the still-cold stove, brought out the teapot and the package of tea. Sophy stumbled with eagerness for cups, saucers, spoons. I poured a little of the boiling water from the kettle into the pot, sloshed it around—I knew the pot must be heated before the tea was made—emptied it, dipped the teaspoon into the box of tea. As I was leveling it off I read in large capitals under the heading of "Instructions" that began with one teaspoon of tea to a cup and one over for the pot. The last, the one with capital letters, read NEVER BRING THE KETTLE TO THE POT. ALWAYS TAKE THE POT TO THE KETTLE.

I dare say to this day they are talking in Penkridge of the heathens from New York who came one day on a barge, and carried a kettle to a teapot.

Mr. Walley arrived as he had promised at half past seven. He was surprised to find us up, awake and dressed but he was more demonstrative over the news we gave him, so distressed in fact Sophy and I found ourselves comforting him and reassuring him it hadn't really mattered. We hadn't minded. We'd been very tired anyway. Hearing myself I broke off suddenly wondering what possessed me other than a beautiful morning, a dear little cottage and the whole of England around us to say such preposterous things as that I had not minded going to bed cold and hungry.

Mr. Walley went at once to a telephone somewhere and came back with the news that Mr. Wyatt from the boatyard at Stone would be with us within the hour bringing a fresh tank of gas if that were needed and equipment for whatever repairs were necessary. "One hour from Stone by car," I murmured to Sophy, and was idiotically thankful I had not known it the night before. Mr. Walley tried the gas tank and the tap at the stove a number of times though he had not waited to do this before telephoning headquarters. He pronounced my diagnosis a correct one. Had he discovered an extra twist or a judicious kick at the tank would have restored the flow I think it highly probable I would have clouted Mr. Walley.

Sophy and I went to the village. We followed the leisurely curves of the road that led us to the shops. No straightening had been done here for speed or thruways. We found fresh bread just arrived at the baker's. A little girl ran to us there from across the way. Her mother, she said, had seen us and thought we might be wanting some new eggs. She had some. I remembered the bowl of sodden beaten eggs on the boat and felt a sudden repugnance to that food. Nevertheless, deciding it was better to be practical than fastidious I followed the messenger to a neat little house set so close to the footpath along the road its front windows bulged out over it. It was only when the child's mother asked me for my basket in which to put the eggs I realized Sophy and I had left our string bags behind. I did not know at that moment Sophy and I had set down a pattern of forgetfulness that by the end of our trip would be the cause of such an accumulation of string bags as pieced together would have made a full-sized hammock. The egg seller could provide no container, of course. I told her I would purchase a basket or bag and return. I rejoined Sophy some yards up the road and on the opposite side. Her arms were filled with purchases half-wrapped in odd and varied coverings. "We forgot our string bags," she informed me, but I made no comment on her talent for the obvious. By the time we reached the butcher's we had acquired bags and a number of things in them including writing paper, stamps and post cards. Each purchase had been made to the accompaniment of delightful, easy, friendly talk. Everyone was not only interested in the reason for our being there and astonished we had come so far, but charmingly pleased we were traveling on their canal. They spoke of it with proprietary pleasure and familiarity though I said to Sophy out of their hearing I doubted any of them had actually traveled on it. The towpath was as close as they came.

The butcher asked if we would wait a few moments. This was the day for his supplies to come in, he said, and the man should be along any moment. I tried without success to picture my Garden Market on Madison Avenue bare of supplies until a wagon should arrive.

The supply truck came within a short time. The interim had provided opportunity for pleasant talk about the menace to respectable people of the motor highways—the speed they encouraged was to the butcher evidence of immorality—of the commendable choice of objective that had induced us to leave America in order to travel on his canal. He called it "our" canal but it was a courtesy adjective.

The talk of our cruise gave me an opportunity to ask if he could spare us any ice. I am glad I made the request. It did not produce ice but it provided for him an insight into the American character I am willing to wager is a topic he still brings up of an evening in the pub. He had just finished telling me of the new installation of cooling pipes with which his establishment had recently been equipped when the meat supplies arrived. The carrier had no sooner come through the door when our new friend after a brief good morning indicated us. "These ladies," he said, "are taking a canal trip. They were asking me for ice. They'd like to carry it along with them." The newcomer eyed us speculatively nodding his head. "American," he said and gave a little bow to us of greeting. He and the butcher looked at each other briefly but it passed for a conversation of some length. I will place another wager that had a verbal exchange taken place it would have been: "Well, I've heard that about Americans. Just like you see in the pictures. Mess up their food and drink with ice. Even on a boat they want it. Fancy."

We left the shop with succulent chops in my string bag. They were wrapped once around in a narrow piece of paper that left either end exposed. The butcher shop was at the end of the main street. Going back along its winding way as we had come Sophy talked happily about the endearing simplicity and ingenuousness of the people we had encountered. "They're so untouched," she said, "so innocent. It's an unsophistication like the countryside itself along these canals. Just meadows and birds and clean air." I interrupted her because we were passing the draper's shop; I had not noticed it when we had first come that way. I was reminded I wanted to buy warm pajamas or night-gown and put or throw away the silly nylons I had brought.

We found a lady keeping shop and I told her what I needed. My children insist no matter how slight the purchase I invariably surround it by a recital of the circumstances that have led to my need, the use to which I intend to put it, and a family biographical sketch. I flout this as preposterous exaggeration. Nevertheless I did tell this shopkeeper something of the misery of the night before, and only in order to make the situation clear to her, I included a brief summary of how we happened to be on the boat and in this vicinity. She was gratifyingly interested. When I had finished she responded with clucking noises of sympathy. She was tall with black hair and dark eyes. She leaned across the counter and patted my shoulder. "What a time you've been having," she said, "but don't mention the word flannel. We haven't seen that since the war. I think we have something that will do you." She turned back to the shelves and presently produced a box from which she extracted a pair of pajamas in a thick material of wide stripes in bright blue and white. I said they would do nicely, hoping fervently no emergency in the night such as a fire would necessitate my quitting the privacy of my own cabin in such a garb. She tore off one sheet of an old newspaper and achieved a bundle of no more concealment than the chops. It was too large to go in either string bag; therefore I was forced to carry it even more conspicuously under one arm. As we turned to leave the shop she leaned across and patted me once more on the shoulder. "Pity," she said, "you haven't anything better than this," indicating my bundle. "A bottle of gin or a man in the bed with you would warm you better." I could think of no reply to this. When we were on the road again I commented to Sophy, "Innocent! Just like the birds and the meadows."

"I should have remembered those innocents we saw yesterday in the hedgerows" was Sophy's answer.

CHAPTER SEVEN

Wε wεrε on our way by eleven o'clock. Mr.
Walley, motorcycle aboard, was at the tiller. The day was
warm, the landscape even more beautiful than the country through which we had traveled the day before. Sometimes we went between woodland patches. The heavy
fringe of trees on either side darkened the water but the
sunlight finding a way along the leaves sprinkled the surface like a seasoning of saffron. The excitement of departure on the day before was behind us. The high-keyed
introductions of yesterday were modulating now to an easy
communication with a friend. The day before had been
like going to a cocktail party, moving quickly from room
to room scarcely pausing on the way to shrill above the
over-all confusion, "Hello. Lovely to see you. How well
you look. Oh, I didn't know you were here." This day was
like the heavenly quiet that comes when a party is over,
the last guest has gone, the doorbell is not going to ring
again. When I have been a hostess this is a time I savor,
though I have wanted to give the party and have enjoyed
it thoroughly; but emptying ashtrays, collecting glasses
almost on tiptoe lest I break the silence, I am aware each

time I repeat this ritual how much each contributes to my enjoyment of the other. The exhilaration of the party sharpens and deepens my sense of a silence that follows but certainly I should not enjoy an unpunctuated stillness.

This trip I was just beginning to sense had something of each. Other trips had been all party. New arrivals continually; the Acropolis in Athens, the ruins at Delphi, Crete, and in Italy the Forum, the Duomo, St. Mark's Square, breath-taking views coming into my recognition one upon another. Here there was one view within sight for an hour or two with scarcely more change than that the arched stone bridge in the distance would be reached and coming nearer I would see its arch so completely shadowed in the water that it became a whole form like an egg. Then presently we would have gone under that bridge but the view ahead would still be the one we had been watching except the bridge was now removed from it. No people crowded this thoroughfare. The water itself was so still it did not even ripple except of our own making as we passed through it. Sitting on the rail in the bow watching this, "God willing," I said to myself, "it will be like this tomorrow and tomorrow," and I went in to prepare elevenses for Mr. Walley.

When I carried the refreshment out to the stern Mr. Walley was telling Sophy about barge people. He stopped courteously in self-effacement at my arrival, asking only if I would be so kind as to let the tea stand in the pot a little longer to "draw." Sophy halted me when I started to pour a cup for her. She would take hers like Mr. Walley, she told me. When he indicated the proper moment had come, I had long since finished my own portion. "Noo then," Mr. Walley advised Sophy, "fill it oop with sugar. That will give ye energy." Sophy prepared the awful brew exactly as he prescribed and pronounced it delicious though I noticed she winced at the first sip. I have a grandson who follows with the same fidelity a baseball hero's endorsement of a breakfast food.

While Sophy and her hero drank their sickening stuff I urged him to tell more about the canal folk. I had learned Mr. Walley was born on a narrow boat but he told us now both his parents and his grandparents had come into the world in the same locale and also his own wife. Mr. and Mrs. Walley had broken from tradition so far as a house on the edge of the canal at Newport and Mr. Walley's transfer of occupation from barge running to maintenance work on the waterways. In his telling the transfer became a bold striking-out for independence regarded with incredulity by his barge friends. Nevertheless they had remained his friends and he assured us there was not a family on any canal in England he did not know. Word of their activities and their welfare was passed along the routes as boats passed or met in locks. It was a party line that never went dead. The children, Mr. Walley admitted, did not have much schooling, though he himself, he emphasized with some pride, had been put ashore and sent to school because his parents were unusually ambitious. He had been permitted to remain until he was eleven years old. There were not many, he gave us to understand, who had enjoyed this privilege.

Girls did not bring a good return if you educated them. The most you could get after their schooling was about three years of work and then they were likely to marry and move to another barge. All boat people, he said, felt sorry for a man with a family of daughters. Not much chance of his being able to put something by. Sophy wanted to know about the system of pay or wages. She is always interested in large areas; I had wanted to ask how they kept the children from falling overboard into the canal. Mr. Walley answered that starting from a basic wage scale the potential of earning depended on the number of loads carried. For this reason every barge man raced to make delivery at a specific point, load up in the shortest possible time and start out again. Therefore, with a family aboard capable of helping he could work very nearly the clock around apportioning the shifts. A wife was a good hand at the tiller and the boys or girls could operate the locks but if a man had only girls they would only give him a few years and a man and a wife could not hold to such a full schedule, so dropping behind they would make a poor living.

Carrying the dishes in to wash I realized I was humming Gershwin's "A Woman Is a Sometime Thing," and bridled at my seeming to fall in with Mr. Walley's estimate of her instability.

We lunched on the boat as we moved along. Mr. Walley had suggested that we not tie up because we had made a late start and he wanted to berth us that night at Norbury. He ate his omelet from a plate beside him at the tiller but requested a cheese sandwich with the bread thick instead of a salad. Anything green he explained was not to his fancy.

This was not the first time I had eaten a meal while in motion; I have endeavored to keep a cup of tea from sloshing over on train and plane, I have munched sandwiches in a car with the same purpose as this, to reach a destination without pause. I have never counted any of these occasions a pleasure in itself but lunch that day was an exquisite delight. We traveled at our usual pace of about three miles an hour. We watched from the open windows in the cabin reeds along the bank bow toward us as our ripples reached them, moorhens in their nervous activity, a blue heron lazily quitting a tree only as we came abreast of it and then lighting on the bank a few yards ahead of us.

"Each time I see a heron land," I told Sophy, "I think of Grandfather Kimbrough's chauffeur Hubert. Hubert never graduated completely from the horse to the Pierce Arrow. Whenever he put on the brake he rose a little in his seat and leaned back as though he were pulling the reins. I always expected to hear him say 'whoa,' and I half expect it from a heron."

We were in Norbury by seven o'clock tied up at a proper dock, not staked to the bank as we had been the night before. We were startled to find ourselves in the midst of work yards. Mr. Walley told us Norbury was a junction and the headquarters in the south of the canal company. What we saw were the materials for canal repairs. There were bricks, iron girders probably for the locks and in the canal itself, that widened here into a basin, was a small fleet of work boats. At the far end of the work yard a long, low wooden building evidently housed the offices of the company; it bore an identifying sign across the front. Mr. Walley walked there and returned with a man who helped remove the motorcycle from our stern. Mr. Walley put on a leather helmet and was transformed almost instantly from a placid navigator to a highway menace. The engine roaring, he wove a path in and around the piles of material at a hair-raising speed and disappeared across the bridge with a final wave of his hand in our direction.

A few minutes after his departure, we had a caller. We saw him come from a charming house set back in a fenced lawn beyond the dock. When he reached the gate we recognized Mr. Lloyd, the Superintendent of Maintenance whom we had met at Stone. He told us his wife had gone up to London for a meeting of the Women's Institute and had asked him to tell us how sorry she was not to be at home when we arrived. I was still unable to make the adjustment from the solitude of the canals to the realization we were actually not out of communication with places and people and so I was surprised to learn anyone knew we were coming to Norbury and almost as astonished to know someone from Norbury had traveled up to London that day and would return the following. Mr. Lloyd asked us to dine with him, adding he was taking care of the children. The tone of his parenthesis indicated considerable harassment. When he included another that one small boy had disappeared on his pony though it was bath time and he must be found, Sophy and I exchanged a look of mutual parental understanding.

This was no time to have guests for dinner. We found it easy to persuade him we would like to be excused, preparations for our dinner were already underway and we wanted to go to bed early.

As we were eating dinner we saw Mr. Lloyd pass along

the dock. He was holding the reins of a pony. He looked hot, a little disheveled and more than a little grim. The small boy on the pony had pink cheeks, yellow curly hair and an expression of some anxiety. He was looking at his father, his father was looking straight ahead, neither was speaking to the other.

All the lights we could see in their house were on when we went to bed; Mr. Lloyd was evidently still endeavoring to bathe and bed his family. Each of us took to her bunk a filled hot-water bottle. I wore my blue-and-white-striped pajamas.

Before leaving the next morning we telephoned Madame Pandit in London. In London the plan had been that she would join us the middle of the week and continue through the weekend. We were to let her know how far we had traveled and where she could catch up with us. To our dismay we learned she was quite ill with the Asian flu. The arrival of this malady had made news in the London papers before we left but it had not reached epidemic proportions. Madame Pandit we learned had caught it from some Indian members of a delegation arriving in preparation for the Prime Ministers' Conference. Several of the delegation had succumbed to the flu shortly after their meeting with Madame Pandit and it was obvious she in turn had caught it from them. She was not so ill we were assured as to cause alarm but unable certainly to come to us at any time on our trip. This was a disappointment; we had talked in London with such high anticipation of this holiday for her.

From the same shed on the dock in Mr. Lloyd's office I put in a call to my daughter in Paris and waiting for its completion looked at the office equipment and marveled again at the British talent for being uncomfortable. A small stove in one corner was obviously the only source of heat, straight wooden uncushioned chairs the complete seating equipment. There was not even an armchair before the flat table that was the office desk. The only concession to comfort I could see was a teapot on an electric plate and beside it a cup, saucer and spoon.

I would not have counted so preposterous a call in New York from New Delhi as I considered talking to the Rue de Courcelles from a dock at Norbury.

There was very little difficulty about making the connection once the telephone operator and I had reached a mutual understanding that when I said "long distance" I was not telling her how far it was to Paris, and when she said "trunk" she was not inquiring about my luggage, but telling me the appellation of "long distance" in England. When presently after a series of clangs and roars I heard a voice say " 'allo, 'allo" I knew we had crossed the Channel. When the same voice had demanded that the English operator and I separately repeat several times the Paris number required, and when she had let us know with a sharp *"comment?"* at each repetition her contempt for our accent, I knew we had reached a Parisian autocrat. Shortly after came the voice of my own child saying " 'allo, 'allo, *j'écoute"* and then a more familiar "Hi, Mommy, where *are* you?"

Returning along the dock, the call completed, I ruminated on the power children have for splitting the personality of a mother. Diamond cutters, rock crushers, pile drivers are as thumbtacks by comparison with the clean

93

rending in two that tots can accomplish from the moment of their birth to the day of our departure. Every woman, I am willing to assert, likes to "get away," the farther away the better she likes it; and yet every woman who is a mother, I am equally willing to assert, wants with equal urgency when she is away, to return to her children in some manner of communication. She has to be assured all is well and by that reassurance be eased of the nagging discomfort that makes her wonder why on earth she wanted to leave home in the first place. Now I was whole again. The group in Paris was having a happy time with my stepmother still there, they had heard from my other daughter in America; the family was intact and happy. I could go farther away.

During the morning we went through the Tyrley Locks, five of them, one after another, strenuous work for Sophy and Mr. Walley as she mentioned a number of times, even calling me into service. She was also kind enough to tell me after we had gone through the first two there were three more to come so I had opened and closed windows only twice around. The narrow lane of water had brought us down from the peak lock through dark woods, steep banks, a landscape unlike any we had seen before and then out again into gentle, rolling meadows and finally a widening of the channel into a basin and a dock.

We were at Market Drayton at noon. We walked the mile or so to the village and found all the shops closed until two. We were glad of an excuse to fill the pause with a hot lunch. We ate well at the Corbet Arms.

At the first shop we visited after lunch, with a head of lettuce and a bunch of radishes in hand and nothing around either of them, we remembered we had forgotten to bring the string bags. Sophy put this errand in my charge together with the lettuce, radishes and subsequent marketing. She must visit the wine shop she assured me to replenish her shoebag supplies. Afternoon closing time was not far off. She must not delay. I dare say she was right and I am always grateful for her efficiency as wine steward but on the pavement when we had parted I wondered if the ignominy of the muddy provisions I held awkwardly in hand had contributed to her sense of urgency. I purchased two string bags and more provisions. I found a bookshop with a glorious supply of paperback English mystery stories, my favorite reading on a trip and the English variety my favorite of the product.

The butcher's was the last shop I visited and both bags were already full. The moment I asked for a steak the butcher and I were involved in a vocabulary difficulty. Sirloin, Porterhouse, the only words I knew, caused him to shake his head doubtfully. It is my instinct to resort to pantomime at a language barrier I am unable to cross, but at the moment my hands were in the air to indicate the size I wanted I was baffled by my ignorance of the part of my person on which to place them. I did not know on what area of a steer live or dead a steak is anatomically located and furthermore I had a slight misgiving there could be an indelicacy in my identification should I guess the source. The butcher was tactful and resourceful. He staggered from his locker room to the counter with the greater part of a creature across his shoulders and, unloading it on a slab, indicated a variety of steak possibilities. I chose one but he flinched when I indicated the thickness I wished it cut. For the folk he served, he told me, this would be more in the nature of a roast, and I was abashed at having displayed once more American profligacy. When I asked him to grind the tail, he had been about to wrap the whole in a piece of paper the size of a lady's pocket handkerchief. He let this go, put both hands on the counter and looked across at me with a bewilderment I would display if someone addressed me in Polish. "Grind the tail?" he repeated as carefully as if he were pronouncing the syllables for the first time. "I'm afraid I don't know what you mean by that. I wouldn't be able to do it."

"Why?" I asked. "You have a machine, haven't you, for chopping or grinding up meat?"

"Oh yes, certainly," he answered with some pride. "We have a fine chopper for sausage."

"Then," I told him and realized I was forming my syllables as carefully as he had done, "would you be so kind as to cut away from the fat that strip of meat at the end of the steak, put it through your chopping machine and then pack it again in the same place?"

He did this obligingly but with the silence of a man who has received a shock and is endeavoring to absorb it. As he patted the ground meat into place I said conversationally, "That part of the steak is tough but when it is ground it's delicious. I don't like to have any part wasted." There was a considerable pause. The butcher replaced the handkerchief-sized paper, put his hands on the counter and leaned toward me again. "I've learned something," he said. "I'm going to tell my customers about that. I thank you for the suggestion." He shook his head incredulously.

"But," he added, "you tell me you do it to avoid waste. A saving as you might say."

I left in the butcher shop a man drowning in confusion. I wonder if he has been able to convince his friends that an American who bought a steak so thick, and I am sure he holds up his fingers so that everyone in the room at the pub can see, had the little piece at the end especially fixed so as not to waste anything. She said it was more economical that way. Those are his words I am sure and I think I know the way he ends his story. He says, "There's an American for you."

I left him in his shop and his sausages with him. He had done his best to persuade me to buy some out of his own grinding machine. He had recommended them highly. As proper a flavor as I would find anywhere he had assured me. From what I had read in English novels about good eating I knew Mr. Walley would savor a nice sausage with his tea but, though I did not tell their creator so, I considered them revolting and I would have none of them. I quitted the shop with a large steak mostly bare cradled in one arm. There were passersby who gave it more than sufficient scrutiny to corroborate the story the butcher would tell.

Before leaving the Corbet Arms I had asked the proprietor if a taxi were available to take us and our supplies back to our boat. He had assured us with some pride it was a very simple thing to arrange. It would be waiting for us at the door at three o'clock. When Sophy and I had departed we had both thought her purchases would be heavier than mine and therefore it would be easier for me to return to the inn and stop for her at the wine shop.

Neither she nor I had estimated I would have two bags full and a steak on the arm.

The taxi was waiting as the landlord had promised. He had not mentioned what the vehicle would be and in my simplicity or perhaps lack of it I had supposed taxis to be much the same in any town. In Market Drayton a taxi is the school bus, of a size to accommodate at least thirty children. It accommodated me nicely but it surprised Sophy considerably when we drew up alongside her and her bottles at the curb, the shop behind her closed. It surprised her so much I had to work my way from the far side, across the wide seat to bang on the window, press my face against it and establish my identity before she would even take cognizance of the fact this equipage was stopping for her.

We covered the remaining distance to our dock at a bounding pace that flung Sophy and me and our provisions into clamorous communion. The driver, friendly and ready with talk about the community, explained he was in a bit of a hurry because he must be back at the school when the children came out and there was not much time. The activity required of Sophy and me to keep the bottles and other supplies from collision or breakage did not give us much time for conversation, but at the dock I did detain the driver when we finished unloading. It had been stupid of me, I told him, not to have thought of this while we were in the town but if he knew somewhere we could get ice I would ride back with him, pick it up and ask him to drive me out once more when he had delivered the children. He had been at the point of leaving but he put on the brake, even turned off the engine, rested his arms across the open window beside him, looked out into space and after some time answered me.

"I can't say as I'm altogether familiar with the place being that I've only lived at Market Drayton for fourteen years but in that time I've seen no ice that I remember of."

CHAPTER EIGHT

Sophy and I feasted that night at Audlem on steak, peas, a salad of lettuce, tomatoes and cucumbers, and thanked Providence, the butcher at Market Drayton and my persistence for the steak. We needed it. We had come down into a green valley in the afternoon by way of twenty-two locks, one so close upon the other it had been like going down a flight of stairs. Though the experience of a lock is always fascinating twenty-two of them are wearying. When we came through the last of them Sophy and I were tired though Mr. Walley gave no sign of it. He still had a distance to go on his motorbike.

When I said this aloud, he was preparing to tie up the *Venturer* for the night. He had jumped ashore carrying a mallet and a long iron spike that was our portable mooring post. He laid these on the ground, caught the rope Sophy threw him and answered me.

"Look back there," he said pointing. "Here's a barge woman coomin' through towing. She has the right to be tired; aye, but she'll not thank ye should ye say ye're sorry for her."

Sophy and I looked where he directed. A woman with

a slight figure was about to pass us. She was pulling a full-size commercial barge. A little boy and a dog walked beside her. She carried the rope over her shoulder and held in both hands, straining so low we could not see her face. Mr. Walley hailed her by name. She released one hand and waved, turning her head so that we saw her face was lined, dirty, but young.

Sophy and I were indignant. Sophy expostulated.

"Is that woman running a barge alone, and without an engine?"

Mr. Walley laughed.

"Oh no," he said. "That's but the butty boat. Her man will be coomin' soon. He's on the main barge with the engine. It draws the butty behind. But there's no room in the locks for the two of them. So he separates the butty and sends it ahead with his woman on the tow. Once she gets started, it's not so heavy poolin'. A boat will move along under its own momentum. Her man follows; then if anything goes wrong he hasn't left her behind. He'll be there to fix it. He's watching out for her."

I made no comment.

Sophy and I were just finishing dinner when we were startled by a knock on the door of the stern cabin. A woman's voice followed immediately asking our permission to tie up just behind us. I hurried to open the door and asked the caller to come in. She followed me back to the main cabin, explaining she had just arrived, was cruising alone and not awfully keen on spending the night in an isolated place. In the light of our middle cabin where the electricity was on I saw she was young, rather stocky with a pleasant face, friendly eyes and smile, and her manner was charming. Sophy with quick perceptiveness asked if she had eaten, adding we were just finishing, there was plenty to share and with all those locks behind her surely she was too tired to cook dinner. After a moment's hesitation our caller admitted this. If we would allow her to wash, and she would be quick, she would accept our invitation gratefully. She returned a few minutes later carrying a portion of a yellow cake and a jug of milk. The only distinction the cake could boast, she said, was that she had baked it on her boat. The milk, she assured us, was quite safe, because the jug had just been scalded. When I asked if she would like with her piece of steak a little of the ground meat that remained, she said she would like very much to try it, though she had never seen let alone tasted it before. When I told her this was what we called hamburger, I might have been offering her a slice of the Empire State Building; they represented to her equal landmarks of America. I assured her this was not like the ancient Chinese original method of obtaining roast pork by burning down the house with the pig in it. It was not necessary in our country to buy an entire steak in order to obtain hamburger. To have it included was simply a measure of economy in order not to have any of the meat wasted. Her surprise at an American's use of the word and practice of economy was only slightly less marked than the butcher's had been. Her friendliness gave me courage to say aloud an opinion I had been muttering to myself in the galley as I threw out provisions that had spoiled. In the department of food, British housewives are not so thrifty as we. Because of poor or no refrigeration they waste time and energy in daily shopping. They are even more wasteful of food. It must either be eaten within a short time of its purchase, or thrown out. There is no keeping the leftovers that dapple an American refrigerator until they are gathered into a casserole or a Waring Blendor.

I had not miscalculated the friendliness of our visitor. She was not offended.

By the end of the evening I counted her unexpected visit one of the happiest surprises that had occurred on any trip. Like Mr. Walley she knew the canals and the people on them at first hand, but she had also a background of sophistication and education that had provoked an intellectual curiosity about their history and traditions.

A few years earlier, she told us, she had decided to take up the profession of nursing but long before that she had become a cruising enthusiast. During her nurse's training course she had taken her holidays exploring the canals as we were doing, but she went alone on her own boat. This holiday marked the completion of her training course and at its end she would take up her first post in social service work, probably directed toward the welfare of the barge people, since she had come to know them so well.

The more she came to know them, she said, the more she was inclined to believe the legend they were Gypsies from Central Europe. Their features and their coloring apart from the tan superimposed by an outdoor life were not Anglo-Saxon. Their love and use of bright colors in dress and in the decoration of their barges had a strong Gypsy and Middle European flavor. A good number of the women, she said, had pierced ears and wore in them large gold hoops, and this was not British adornment. Looking from the broad stout shoes of our guest to the full heavy cotton short skirt above woolen stockings (no such frivolity as slacks) a tailored warm blouse and over it a heavy double-breasted coat like a sailor's pea jacket, short hair and ruddy tanned face of fine features and no trace of powder or lipstick, I found it easy to believe gold hoops in pierced ears were the equivalent of a stamp NOT MADE IN GREAT BRITAIN.

No out-and-out British boats, she pointed out further, would be decorated in such bright colors as the barges were painted, nor in such patterns. "Notice the castles," she said, "in their landscapes painted on the doors. They're not English, they're castles on the Rhine or somewhere in Middle Europe." All this painting, she told us, had been done at Market Harborough and the adornment was not only on the barges themselves but on the actual cooking utensils, teapots and water carriers, broad, short-handled scoops used to dip water from the canal for cooking. I saw Sophy echo my involuntary shudder. So did our guest. "They drink it too," she said grimly, "but they seem to have developed an immunity to the germs that must be there."

She urged us to look for an elaborate decoration sometimes but not always found on the stern of a barge. This decoration she said was done in large plaits of rope chalked white. Hanging loose from this in long shredded strands there was also sometimes a facsimile of a horse's tail. She had never been able to learn the reason or origin of this unless it was a symbol of the fact that originally all barges were horse drawn. She hoped we would be able to visit the cabin in a barge; it would not be easy to accomplish,

but perhaps Mr. Walley might manage it. We would find, she said, the living space of the entire family would be eight feet long and seven feet wide. Immediately on the left of the cabin doors we would see the cook stove that also provided heat and on this at any hour of the day a pot of tea brewing. Next to the stove would be a tall cupboard, the door painted in the same patterns of castles and flowers as the door panels of the boat itself. This cupboard door, she said, was on a hinge so that, opened and unhooked, it became a table for eating like the one in our own cabin. Across from this cupboard there would be, she told us, a bench. This was the only place one could sit and, at night, was a bed for the children. Across the width of the cabin at one end would be the bed for the bargeman and his wife, separated from the children's by a pair of curtains. This is where a bargeman and then his children are born and this is where they will die. Until they can be trusted not to toddle off the side of the barge into the water the little ones are kept during the daytime in a hammock slung the length of the cabin under its roof. "That is why," our visiting nurse explained and shook her head angrily, "you will see barge people with shocking malformation of the legs, bowed and twisted by actually living in a hammock. That is also why," she continued, "most of these people can neither read nor write." She laughed at herself a little. "I don't mean because the children live in hammocks, I mean because, except for the times of loading and unloading at a dock, their lives are spent on a boat. However," she added and her face became stern, "we're changing all that. Now there is regular and periodic health inspection and the children must be put ashore for a

certain amount of schooling. They don't take kindly to it I must say," she admitted, and grinned engagingly. "They can hide like an animal of the woods when word goes around an official is coming to learn the number of children on board and their ages. The parents are no help except to the children. If there are girls or boys of school age the parents want them for work. They help in the towing as well as the loading and unloading and sometimes you'll see a little fellow so small he can scarcely see over the top but he's working the tiller." She told us too about the butty boats.

I said I imagined the cabins must be unspeakably dirty. Such a small space with almost any number of people living in it couldn't possibly be kept clean. Our guest denied this vehemently.

"They're spotless," she assured me. "Every barge woman has a collection of brass! Pitchers, jugs, kettles, bands and safety chains around the chimney of the stove, knobs on the doors, and every piece of it is gleaming. They all have lace curtains at the windows starched and white. The minute they're away from the coal yard and on the water again a barge woman is washing her curtains and polishing her brass. Every one of them has a collection of souvenir plates too. They hang in racks on the wall and there is a tremendous rivalry over who has the largest number. Sometimes you'll find a really beautiful piece, but most of them say Birmingham, Reading or whatever town the barge has visited, and I'm sure the only reason a barge woman visits the town and goes so far away from the water is to buy a souvenir plate."

While Sophy and I were still asking questions our guest

stood up. She must go, she said. She had had a long day's
run and was a little tired. Remembering the locks, I chalked
this up as another triumph of British understatement. She
thanked us with fervor for having fed her and said she
would see us again in the morning before she left. "Are
you by any chance going into the village to bath?" Sophy
and I were startled and looked inquiringly at each other
and at her. "Is there a lake?" I asked.

"A lake?" she echoed in evident bewilderment. "Oh
dear me no, not that I know of." We were obviously at
cross purposes. "Well, where does one swim?" Sophy asked.
Again we had an echo. "Swim? I shouldn't think one could
swim."

I tried this time. "I thought you suggested bathing."

Again she informed us of something. "Oh, I mean a
bath," she explained. "It's quite customary you know on
a cruise. You take your towel and soap and a sponge with
you to an inn. They're glad to let you have the use of a
tub for a shilling. Perhaps you'll join me." It seemed to
me an unusual invitation, but I did not say so.

We saw her off the stern of our boat, but a few minutes
later we heard her call at the aft-cabin door. She came in
with a large oil-burning lantern and a book of information
and regulations about the canals, issued she said to members of the Canal Association.

"Do keep both of these," she urged; "they may come in
handy, and when you come back to Stone just leave them
there in my name at the boatyard, I'll pick them up on my
next cruise. By the way," she added, "here's my name and
where I live." She handed me a piece of paper. "I do wish
you'd go up there for as long as you like, I think you'd

enjoy that part of the country and I'd love to put you up. I shan't be there, but my old nurse keeps it going! She'd be glad to look after you. Good night again."

When she had gone I read from the paper: Muriel Ritchie. Grange Farm Cottage, West Burton, then a name I couldn't read, North Yorkshire.

Sophy and I stared at each other. "I give up," she said. "They say the British are aloof, almost unapproachable. Can you imagine any American inviting total strangers to stay as long as they liked, in a house where the hostess wouldn't even be at home to count the silver?" She called a final comment when we were each in bed. "And *she* was surprised by a little piece of hamburger."

CHAPTER NINE

W<small>E DID</small> not join Miss Ritchie the following morning for a bath at the inn. I went shopping in the village and when I returned she had gone. The shopping had taken a considerable time because I was in search of a potholder. In my simplicity I had thought this kitchen accessory as easily available as say a fork or a spoon. I began asking for it in the shop where I made my first purchases of food. I am chagrined to admit actually I had made my initial inquiry at the shop at which I purchased two string bags, in lieu of the ones I had forgotten to bring.

No one knew what I meant by a potholder. Each time I explained, with what I considered vivid pantomime, that a potholder was a sort of pad by means of which one could remove cooking vessels from the fire without burning one's hands, I knew from the expression on the face of my listeners my audience was not with me. The first time the ironmonger's was suggested I flouted the idea. But when it had been repeated in several establishments I gave in and visited that shop. I am convinced now the

111

average inhabitant of an average English village regards any time-saving or mechanical device as something outlandish and that the ironmonger's is a museum of oddities. The ironmonger's was conspicuously the most up-to-date store in the community. It stood on a corner with large show windows on two sides so that the whole interior could be seen from the street and was brightly illuminated with neon lights. My impression when I entered was there were more advertising placards of miraculous devices than merchandise itself. I had a feeling the shop owner shared in a practical way my impression that his townsfolk were not so much novelty-conscious as novelty-suspicious. He was therefore not going to invest in the actual merchandise until he had mellowed sales resistance by a preliminary exhibition of alluring posters.

He waited on me identifying himself as the proprietor, and in answer to my congratulations on the splendor of his establishment told me it was recently opened, and added, somewhat anxiously I thought, he hoped to make a go of it. When I inquired for a potholder he responded after only a moment's hesitation by an invitation to accompany him on a tour of the gallery of posters. He paused before each one and read its text meticulously from beginning to end, aloud. It was not until the third selection had been completed I realized he was endeavoring to find in its context the word potholder. I explained what I hoped to purchase had nothing to do with a dishwasher, a vacuum cleaner nor an electric grill. It was merely something with which to hold a pot in order not to be burned. He was immediately and obviously relieved. This was something he actually had in stock. He found a ladder and by means of it climbed to a high shelf, bringing down from there a box that seemed to me large and heavy for the object of my search. I concluded it must contain a gross or more. What it contained was a small metal stand on three legs. He lifted it from the container and set it on the counter before me. "What you want," he said, "is a trivet; that's what we call it." The image of my wrapping this around the handle of a saucepan provoked a babble of incoherence by which I endeavored to explain I wanted to hold in my hand the thing I sought. It was a pad, it was made of cloth. At the word cloth two women clerks who had followed us at a respectful distance, but within hearing range, hurried simultaneously into our immediate proximity.

"What the lady wants," one of them ventured, "is an oven cloth."

"That's it," the other one corroborated.

Help had come, the Marines had landed. I wanted to kiss the brightly rouged cheek of each of those peroxide beauties. "That must be it," I told them eagerly, "you call it an oven cloth. The thing that protects your hands from being burned when you are taking a pan off the stove."

"That's right," they said in unison, nodding their wood-shaving curls.

Reaching my goal made me wildly profligate. "I'll take two," I told them. Each feminine countenance saddened and the proprietor shook his head. "We don't sell such things," he said, "I'm sorry."

I was the one to apologize, I told him, for causing him such trouble by my own stupidity and the misfortune of vocabulary differences between American and British speech. I had been directed to him because I had not made myself understood elsewhere. Would he be so kind as to tell me where I *should* go?

One of the blondies spoke. "Oh, you couldn't go anywhere," she said, "not to buy an oven cloth."

I do not know a way of measuring stages of bewilderment but I can assert this statement produced in me an acute confusion.

"If women use oven cloths as you call them where do they get them?" I inquired and realized my condition was inducing me to pronounce each syllable meticulously.

"One makes them," Blondie answered, "at home. And sometimes for church bazaars."

I plodded back along the road from the village to the canal. At the curve where a steep footpath branched off and staggered to the towpath I paused a moment to shift the heavy string bags before I made the descent. In that pause I saw below me tied up just ahead of the *Venturer* a long barge and along the side near me in giant letters the label ICE-BOAT. I whistled and I yelled. I think I even jigged a little on that precarious summit. Sophy popped out through the doors of the aft cabin. "What on earth's the matter with you?" she called.

"Look at that," I bawled, swinging the string bags like Indian clubs. "Look what's here. *Ice, ice*. A whole boat load of it. We can get all we want." Sophy jumped to the towpath and stared in the direction I was indicating. Mr. Walley had arrived in my absence and was working over the engine. At the sound of our clamor he straightened up, came to our side of the boat, leaned far out and looked.

"That's right," he said, "it's the ice boat. Of course she's not working now, but she's a fine sight to see in the winter when the ice is thick and she's breaking it through and cracking it up."

We were well on our way and I had put all our provisions in the cupboard before I spoke again.

The day, like the ones before it, was sunny and warm. There were larks in the sky, water lilies on the water's surface, fish beneath, and blue heron on the watch for them. When one of these anglers was about to make a catch our approach did not disturb, it did not even distract him. When he left the scene, it was not because we were abreast of him, but that a wiggling fish was firmly pinched in his long beak. Only moorhens behaved hysterically; the swans showed an aggressiveness that evoked from me behavior not unlike that of the moorhens. They and I left the immediate scene with squeaks and flutters.

I was covering up such a retreat by pretending I had hurried in to prepare elevenses when I happened to look out the window over the sink. I saw motor cars seeming to emerge from beneath us onto a highway and others from the highway disappearing under our boat. I ran across the cabin to look out the other side. The same phenomenon was in sight. It was extraordinary to view a highway when we had been floating through meadows, but to have it beneath us was out of reason. I returned to the bow, confused.

"I thought you would come back," Sophy told me. "We're on a cast-iron aqueduct. That's the Chester road down there, and over there is the Vale of Nantwich."

The channel on the viaduct is so narrow I had not seen

from the windows the side boundaries of the construction that was carrying us. I count it an eerie experience to cross a bridge that is filled with water, and look down on motor traffic where a river should be.

We were in Nantwich by half past two in the afternoon. There is a sizable yacht basin here, and when we arrived we found a number of motor cruisers at anchor. The owner of one of these was tying up his boat at a dock as we arrived. He strolled across to greet us and, when he came close enough to permit recognition, addressed Mr. Walley by name, with no observable evidence of surprise. Mr. Walley responded with a corresponding lack of demonstrativeness but leaned out the stern of our boat, and the two shook hands. Sophy and I happened to be there at the moment; I was thinking how wide Mr. Walley's acquaintanceship was since it seemed to extend beyond barge people to holiday cruisers, when Mr. Walley said, "This is my first cousin and we're fine pals too. It's about three years since we've seen each other, eh George?"

"Aye," George answered. "Coom abaht nicely, this meeting."

Not wanting such exuberance stemmed by our presence Sophy and I suggested she and I explore the town and allow the two cousins to enjoy their reunion. When we had changed from slacks to dresses and come on the dock Mr. Walley with his relative was talking to a group of men a little distance away gathered around a gasoline pump. Seeing us he approached, shaking his head. The news was not good, he told us, of conditions on the canal. The water was not coming in as rapidly as had been hoped. We might get stranded. Therefore, in his opinion it would be good if we stayed overnight allowing that many more hours for filling. Agreeing to this it occurred to Sophy and me we might enjoy the change of a night on shore. Mr. Walley assured us it was quite safe to leave the boat untended, but he would stay until we learned what accommodations were to be had.

We walked to the town, but we could not hurry. The distance was perhaps a little over a mile and within every few yards was something that halted and delighted us. Rounding a bend of the country road from the docks we were on a street almost entirely of another century. Jacobean houses, timber-built of blackened oak in superb criss-cross pattern with whitewash interstices between, edged the walk, their upper gables frowning over it. Such dwellings as were not of this period sat behind gardens in such enthusiastic bloom as to have lost all pattern or coherence; roses scrambled over fences that lined the walk. We found several hotels in the town proper, but chose the Crown because it was timbered like the houses we had passed. We had some difficulty in being admitted because the time of our arrival was during "closing hours." In England when a bar in an inn observes closing rules, the entire inn is locked up, probably allowing the proprietor and staff to enjoy an afternoon nap. Banging on the main door of the street brought no response. We found a side entrance in a courtyard and hallooing and beating on this eventually brought admittance and a pleasant conversation with the owner and his wife, an attractive couple. We were to discover many inns we visited are run these days by ex-servicemen who, in their words, could not stick a job in an office after the war, but wanted something that allowed one to move about and not be restricted in hours and space.

There was a room available. We signed the register, came out on the street, secured a taxi and returned to the dock. Mr. Walley was waiting for us and at the moment of our arrival was talking to a young couple we had seen pull in as we were dressing to go ashore. We joined the conversation and learned they were on a holiday and were discomfited by the news of the shortage of water ahead. They were endeavoring to decide whether to risk it or turn back, though the objective of this long-planned cruise had been Wales. I was sympathetic but Sophy was acutely distressed. I recognized the reason for the shade of difference in our response was that I am not only somewhat indifferent about achieving a specific objective on a trip, I am not always sure what it is; whereas Sophy, plotting and charting the journey, looks toward a specific end much as an Alpine climber aspires to the summit of the Matterhorn. She promptly invited the young people to return to the town with us for tea and they accepted gratefully. They had been told, they said, it was no use trying to push on that afternoon anyway and if they stayed on board they would simply brood over what they ought to do.

Sophy and I packed small bags hurriedly; we had asked the taxi to wait. Mr. Walley told us he had decided to spend the night on the *Venturer*. It would give him time to make further investigation of conditions ahead. On the way into town we learned our guests were Mr. and Mrs. David Palmers and from the taxi driver that the Churche house would be pleasant for tea. I demurred at this, thinking the annex to a church scarcely the spot I would select to bring cheer to disappointed holiday makers. Happily and remarkably, because it is not my custom to keep objections to myself, I made no protest aloud.

The Churche house is the excellently preserved residence of Mr. Churche, who was a prosperous citizen of the community in the sixteenth century. It is a half-timbered structure with magnificent oak paneling. Its façade includes four gables, each delicately and intricately carved. The paneling in the interior is equally handsome.

The present owner has been able to afford its careful restoration by having tea served and antiques sold. This is commercializing I consider thoroughly commendable; not only because it has made possible such costly preservation, but because undoubtedly its delicious cakes and sandwiches bring a great many people who would not visit a museum. Thanks to this owner who took us on a tour we were cautioned about the elevated doorsills so that we did not plunge from one room into another. We were also told the reason for this difference in level had been to prevent rushes that once covered the floors from being carried by shuffling feet from one room to another. I had not known either until our host told us the origin of the word "chairman" or the phrase "taking the chair." It comes from the furnishings and customs of the period. The master of the house and his lady were the only ones who owned and occupied chairs. The rest of the household, although it shared a community dining table, sat on stools and at a lower level. I learned that a guest of consequence was honored by being invited to "take the chair."

Bathing in a tub filled with hot water is a beautiful custom. I observed it with a prolonged pleasure at the inn when the Palmers had gone to their boat. I terminated it, and rapidly, only when Sophy shouted the news of a tall glass of white wine and soda with two *cubes* of *ice* in it.

Mr. Walley's news next day was not good. The Palmers had left disconsolately, he said, returning the way they had come. He had gone on to Whitchurch and learned we could not make it that day but if we stayed over one more night there should be enough water to carry us. We explored the town during the day and found it charming. We dined at the Cheshire Cat and found it not very enticing but the place served to bring me my first awareness we were in Cheshire. When I deplored the absence of signs along the route such as we have at home—"You are now leaving the State of Connecticut. This is New York" —Sophy speculated perhaps it was the prevalence of signposts at home that was responsible for such map illiterates as I. I did not prolong the discussion but ordered Cheshire cheese and it was delicious.

We slept on the boat and were on our way the next morning around nine. At Hurleston we left the Shropshire Union Canal and turned left—I do not know in what direction left was—into the Llangollen, and it is also known as the Ellesmere, Canal. The inland cruising booklet, called *Cruising on the Llangollen Canal,* says of Hurleston:

Access is gained to the canal by four locks each with an independent chamber separated by a short pound. The lower gates of these locks are in two mitreing leaves,

while the upper end is closed by a single clapping-gate.
Immediately above the locks is the Hurleston Reservoir
with a capacity of some 93 million gallons at full storage
level. Unlike most canal reservoirs it does not receive its
supply from the run-off of a local catchment area but de-
pends for its contents on water passed down the length of
the canal and fed into the reservoir over the weir at
Hurleston. It is thus a balancing reservoir, receiving its
supplies when there is a surplus passing down the canal
and being drawn upon when there is a shortage of water
in the main canal.

What I say of it is: there was no surplus, very little
water and we had to be towed between the locks. These
locks boasted a keeper. He was more of an obstacle than
an assistance because he was not only totally deaf but
churlish about permitting us to go through his locks.
Since his employment depended on the expediting of
boats through this passage I do not know why he was so
reluctant to give us access but he unlocked and then locked
behind us each division before he would move on to the
next, somewhat as though we were passing through private
property and he wanted to make sure we did not make
off with anything valuable. What souvenir we might have
snatched from the sheer bare walls I am unable easily to
conjecture.

We had callers during the afternoon. Mr. Lloyd, last
seen taking home to supper a reluctant little boy on a
pony, and Mr. Hughes, another official of the waterways.
They were uneasy about the lack of progress we were
making and they had reason to be. The water was shallow

and filled with reeds. No matter how slowly Mr. Walley ran the *Venturer,* and we were scarcely moving, he had frequently to stop and upturn the propeller to clean it.

The day was hot. When I prepared elevenses I found the milk had soured. I was reassured when I discovered in the cupboard a lemon I remembered having purchased earlier on the trip, with the silly optimism that somewhere along the nearly two thousand miles of canals in England there would be ice available and I would have a glass of cold tea with lemon in it. I put two slices on the tea tray I carried out to Mr. Walley at the tiller and explained the reason for the substitution. Mr. Walley shook his head at the sight and waved it aside courteously. As he tilted the pot he said, "I'll just take it plain, thank ye"; then leaning toward me he added confidentially, "Lemon twists me bowels." I consider this a phrase with a Spenserian flavor and certainly it left me in no doubt about the effect on Mr. Walley's system of a piece of citrus fruit.

Mr. Walley towed us through Swanley Locks, all three of them. There was not enough water to permit running the engine without danger of being stuck. The country was flat, fertile and hot, not so interesting as landscapes of the other days, but populated by couriers from the Transport Waterways. They came to us on bicycles along the towpath. Sometimes we would find a messenger leaning over a bridge as we approached waiting to call down news of the water situation ahead. We were so removed from any signs of our own times, motor highways, telephone wires, I told Sophy I would not be too surprised if a runner or perhaps a carrier pigeon brought us news of the Battle of Waterloo.

Frequently during the afternoon one of these news bearers would be detained by Mr. Walley to help tow for a stretch. Sophy stood at the tiller steering without benefit of motor. I made and served tea to a sizable number of people though not at the same time. They came and went. I had also given lunch to more than our daily quota. I do not remember a day spent less idly.

Along five o'clock Mr. Walley, who had come on board for his tea, thought he might risk running the motor cautiously. There seemed to be a little more water in this stretch than over the preceding miles. Sophy, relieved of her job at the tiller, jumped to the bank and walked along the towpath. She wanted some exercise she said and called me to share it. I was at the sink washing up the dishes and I answered her through the window with some acidity that the fulfillment of my humble tasks during the day had given me considerably more exercise than I cared for. She walked more briskly than the boat was moving and in a short time was considerably ahead of us. I finished the dishes and went forward to sit on the rail of the bow thankful to be able to assume that position and even more thankful, as I watched her stride, I was not accompanying Sophy. I saw her approach a bridge of a sort we had not seen before. It was so narrow as to allow only one vehicle at a time to cross, and had to be raised by hand to permit a boat to go under. Three little boys were playing on the bank opposite the one on which Sophy walked. They were watching our approach with evident excitement, jumping about and nudging one another. As Sophy came abreast of them the oldest, who was perhaps seven, called out, "We'll open the bridge for you, lady. We're going to open it." I heard her answer something to the effect that this was very nice of them. I saw them run in happy confusion to a long handle like a sweep. They bore down on this, all of them leaning across it, and the bridge slowly began to rise from the other side.

Sophy had moved forward a little, probably in order to see what this simple mechanism was, and stood almost immediately beneath where the planking had been at ground level. Suddenly and simultaneously the children let go, outbalanced by the rising heavy weight. They tumbled to the ground and, like a seesaw released, the end they had been holding flew back up into the air. The thick planking released crashed to the ground and caught Sophy on the side of her head. Had she been standing a few inches nearer the center it would have caught her squarely on top of the head with a result that required no great imagination to conjecture. She was knocked to the ground and rolled down the bank but stopped just before she went into the water and sat up shaking her head groggily. Mr. Walley in the stern had not seen this happen and because the engine was running did not hear me shout.

By a heaven-sent coincidence a courier came toward us on a bicycle along the towpath on the side where the frightened little boys huddled. This was also the side, the starboard, where the tiller was placed, so Mr. Walley could see what was going on there. The cyclist flung himself over the lever or sweep. Mr. Walley during this time had been easing us over to the bank. He jumped off to help with the bridge shouting to Sophy to take the tiller.

By the time I had cracked my head on the doorway of the forward cabin, forgetting in my agitation to stoop, and

124

Vasiliu

reeled from that to the stern to tell Mr. Walley what had happened, he had left the boat and was on the bank. I was alone on the *Venturer* and as far as I knew Sophy was dying of a fractured skull. What with my leaning out to shout incoherently that Mrs. Jacobs had been hurt and my tremulous hands on the tiller it is a wonder I did not finish off Sophy by directing the *Venturer* straight into if not over her. I did drive our vessel into the bank, though providentially a few yards beyond my friend. I rammed the boat so successfully there was no possibility she could move on without us and with the engine running she was becoming more vigorously landlocked every minute. Inasmuch as I had not the faintest idea how to operate the motor when it was running, I certainly had no intimation of how to stop it. I therefore left it to its own machinations and quit the boat by rushing forward again, ducking in the nick of time at the forward cabin and jumping down from the bow. There was no water space to be leapt over. I had eliminated that with the *Venturer*; but I did not land on the bank, I landed on Sophy. Specifically I landed against her, chest to chest, and the impact put her on the back of her head for the second time within perhaps three minutes. Once more she sat up groggily as I removed myself from her and looked into her face with acute anxiety. The first time she had been thrown down she had not made a sound, but the second toss evoked an audible comment.

"What the hell are you doing?" she inquired.

All of us heard her question with clarity because Mr. Walley had returned to the boat, and at that moment shut off the engine. However, I think his comment was an announcement and not an answer, though the gender made it ambiguous.

"She's stook proper," he called.

Sophy flouted my suggestion she might have a fractured skull. She assured the two men she had not been badly hurt and enchanted the little boys by stooping to their level, pushing her hair aside gingerly and revealing a sizable egg.

Mr. Walley said we were close to the village of Wren-bury. It was now five thirty and there would be a bit of work to do before we were afloat again. What Sophy murmured at this I prefer not to remember. He suggested we stop for the night. I was grateful for this suggestion in every aching muscle. I wanted also to remove myself from the boat. I was suddenly not nearly so fond of her as I had been heretofore. I proposed I go into the village as usual for provisions. Sophy insisted on accompanying me though I urged her to lie down in the cabin or on the bank. She flouted this too.

The bicyclist stayed with Mr. Walley. The little boys joined Sophy and me and as we walked along the dusty road past a charming church they asked questions about our trip. Did we eat on that boat and sleep on that boat and where did we eat and sleep when we were not on the boat? I told them in New York. Did they know where that was? No, they did not. I said it was in the United States. No response. I said we were Americans and we lived in America. Again silence, followed unexpectedly by a leap into the air of the middle-sized boy who was perhaps five. On the ground again he seized my right arm with both hands and shook it violently, looking up into my face with excitement. "America?" he said. "United States? That's where Danny Kaye lives." I could not quench such rapture by putting myself the width of a continent from Mr. Kaye's residence. Instead, I edged us closer and closer until in the blissful conjecture of that little boy and his two companions, the Kayes and I are separated only by a garden wall such as the one we were at that moment passing, and frequently we lean across our boundary from either side for neighborly conversation.

CHAPTER TEN

AT NINE o'clock the following morning we were on our way once more. The *Venturer* had been refloated in time for Mr. Walley to eat a hearty dinner the night before. Under the circumstances I had put my all into the preparing of it. In the morning Sophy's cranial egg was conspicuous but less painful, she insisted. Just before our take-off we watched with considerable interest and had some conversation with a young couple who came near us along the bank carrying a kayak. They put this in the water and while the young woman stayed with it the man went away, returning after some time with knapsacks and a few packages. They stowed these carefully, preserving a delicate balance in the little cockleshell, and while they were doing this she explained she and her husband were starting their annual fortnight's holiday, camping out in any weather, but with a concession to rain of a tarpaulin. They had come from London by train, the kayak in the van. They had carried it and their personal belongings from the railroad station.

"Doughty British, sissy Americans," I said as we passed them and waved good-by.

"Speak for yourself" was Sophy's answer as she looked back, wistfully I thought.

Those vacationers were going in the direction from which we had come. We should have done the same thing, but there are only a few places in the canal system in which a large boat can turn around and this was not one of them. Had we been able to turn around we would not have visited Llangollen, but that Saturday, the first of June, was in Mr. Walley's own word 'orrible. Birds sang, flowers bloomed, the sun shone and a light breeze brought us a stench from which we did not escape for three hours. The stench was with us because the owner of a dairy farm had substituted the canal for any other form of drainage or removal of refuse. We traveled through muck and at a pace a tortoise could easily have outrun.

When it became unendurable, and that did not take long, Sophy and I dived below to the cabins, closing all doors and windows. This eliminated the smell but created a temperature not appreciably below a bake oven's. When this became unendurable we emerged to the stern for cooler but certainly not fresh air. What we breathed there was such a swift inducement to nausea we were driven back into the oven. On trips across the plains and desert to the West Coast I have seen prairie dogs popping into and out of their holes. With some difference of habitat and of size, Sophy and I that afternoon might have been members of their family.

On one of our emergences we found Mr. Walley had tied a handkerchief around the lower part of his face. The section above it I noticed was not its usual ruddy color. He told us from behind his bandit mask the farmer responsible for this outrage had been served notice. He was to appear in court very shortly and would certainly have a heavy fine imposed, plus a requirement to clear this area immediately. I expressed a fervent hope he might be jailed as well, preferably in a cell constructed on a bank somewhere along this section. That was as much conversation as I dared risk. With clenched teeth we dived below again. Some time later we thought we heard a sound of voices and not long after that Mr. Walley opened the doors of the aft cabin and called to us.

"We're coomin' oot o' the mook," he said.

We ventured up once more and I took a cautious breath. Never, I think, in my life have I been so aware of the beauty of fresh air. We were still moving slowly. The water was shallow, but it was clear. We could even see fish again. We saw also another courier had arrived. A stocky, ruddy-faced man, medium height, of I should have thought around fifty, was walking alongside us on the towpath, pushing a bicycle. We recognized Mr. Hughes, superintendent of that area. He had come to see how we were doing and report the water was not coming in ahead as fast as they had hoped and we might run into trouble. I started to tell him with some vigor the trouble we had just run through but Sophy kicked me sharply on the shin and wincing I acknowledged this rebuke by cutting off what might have been an elegant oration. I had been brooding some time over what I would say when there was someone to listen; instead I asked Mr. Hughes if he lived nearby. We hoped we had not inconvenienced him. He assured us this visit was part of his routine coverage of the area. He generally averaged he said about thirty-five miles a day. By car, I supposed. Not at all, he told us. A car would be of no use to him because a great part of the canal in his district was some distance from a road. He had to follow the towpaths and used his bicycle. A towpath is a grass-tufted, bumpy passage. I could not have maintained a bicycle seat for more than a few yards. I did not mention this either to Mr. Hughes.

He expressed a little dissatisfaction with the Waterways Association. Sophy broke in with indignant sympathy. It was certainly asking too much she asserted to cover such an area by bicycle. He was surprised. This wasn't what he minded at all he said. It was the wear and tear on the machine. He thought they should pay for a new one when it was necessary that it be replaced. When I timidly asked Mr. Hughes if he didn't find such travel tiring he answered he enjoyed it, adding he was sixty-five years old and had been doing this for well over forty of those years.

Mr. Walley interrupted to say he didn't consider it safe to continue under power. If Sophy would take the tiller, he thought he and Mr. Hughes had better tow for a stretch. For nearly two hours after that, while Sophy steered, Mr. Walley and Mr. Hughes walked the towpath, the rope between them over Mr. Walley's shoulder. Mr. Walley pulled with both hands, the windlass for locks hanging from his coat collar. Mr. Hughes pulled with one hand and with the other guided his bicycle. Ever since Hurleston we had been going uphill. During that period of hard pulling I never saw them stop talking. I could see from the bend of their bodies what effort was required, but the exertion seemingly did not even tax them with a shortness of breath. I pointed this out to Sophy and lest she tell me she was sure she could do it, I went hurriedly up forward and sat in the bow.

Around six o'clock I called to the team on the towpath to ask our prospects for putting in for the night. After a consultation between them I was told prospects were not good. The plan had been to reach Ellesmere in time for dinner ashore but at our rate of travel, and there was no indication of bettering it, this could not be accomplished. Nevertheless both men agreed we should push on to Ellesmere at whatever time we reached it. With the water so shallow it would not be advisable to tie up at the bank and run the risk of settling on the mud. Remembering the settling job I had accomplished the day before I considered it unwise to demur but the prospect did not please. I went to the stern for a consultation with Sophy. I had laid in no supplies for an evening meal. I had even used the last of the bread for tea. There was a tin of soup in the locker, a few potatoes, and the only other nourishment salt, pepper, sugar, milk and tea. We are neither of us, as Sophy pointed out, spirits that subsist on air and dew and certainly Mr. Walley could not be classified in that category. We might be entertaining Mr. Hughes as well. If the water did not allow us to run the motor, it would be disastrous to lose him. I counted it generous of Sophy not to reproach me for an excessive and impractical thrift, and as I told her so, I was mentally estimating how much I could dilute the small tin of soup, and into how small portions allot the potatoes. She interrupted my musing.

"Look over there," she said and pointed to the left.

On the opposite bank, along which the towers were plodding, was a dirt road, and standing squarely in the center of it a covered truck that carried along the side nearer us a beautiful inscription: MEATS. A little away from it on the edge of the bank a man in a butcher's long white coat stood watching our approach. He was only a few yards ahead of us.

Sophy called out, "Have you any meat for sale?" The man on the bank started but answered almost immediately. "The best lamb in Shropshire."

The last I knew we had been in Cheshire. That Mr. Brindley's curves had brought us back into Shropshire again was a surprise to me, but a far greater and happier surprise was the butcher with his cart. Within a minute or two Mr. Walley was back on the *Venturer* at the tiller and Sophy and I were standing on the movable steps at the back of the butcher's wagon, looking at an assortment of meats so delectable to our hungry eyes it surpassed any landscape we had viewed that day. We bought thick chops and we attracted the interested attention of a young woman and her children from a house nearby. She heard me telling the threat of starvation that had hung over us until we saw him—my children maintain it is impossible for me to make the smallest purchase without including a considerable narrative of family circumstances—and offered shyly to sell us some lettuce and radishes from her garden. Tears were in my eyes when I thanked her. When the butcher told me hers was the only house for some distance around and he visited it infrequently because it was out of his way, I wrung his hand that he should have chosen this particular day and hour. When he added it was unusual to see a barge like ours coming along, he had stopped just to see what it might be, I would have invited him to join us on

134

the cruise had I not thought it unlikely he would abandon his van and stock.

My arms filled with beautiful booty, I was about to descend the bank when I heard a shout "Oi, Bill." I looked back and noticed for the first time a bridge across the canal some yards ahead of us. A small van was parked there and on the side nearer us an inscription that carried someone's name (I have forgotten that), but as though the letters had been in gold I shall remember always the identification that followed: BREAD. Evidently the baker was a friend of the butcher's and I loved them both. Had he any bread to sell, I inquired loud and eager.

"Baked at noon today," he answered, "and still warm. I'm just making my last delivery but I've two loaves to spare if you'd like them." If we would like them!

We dined magnificently but Mr. Hughes was not our guest. While Sophy and I were eating in the main cabin, Mr. Walley dining at the tiller, Mr. Hughes was pedaling some portion of the thirty-five miles to his house. There was enough water to permit the engine to be run, though slowly. It was half past ten when we reached Ellesmere, and it was scarcely half an hour later when we were in our beds on the boat.

At eight o'clock the next morning we were on our way again, proceeding nicely under power. The day was fine, the country beautiful, the water not choked with reeds. If we were not singing when we reached a lock at half past eleven it was only because each of us is aware her singing voice does not contribute to the aesthetic pleasure of the other. We were surprised at Upper New Martin lock to see a lockkeeper's house, but considerably more surprised when a lockkeeper shot out its door waving his arms and yelling to us to stop where we were. The news he brought was the greatest surprise of all.

"Don't open them gates," he urged, "there's not a drop of water t'other side. Dry as a rock she be. You've coom as far as you're going."

A royal edict with the crown seal and a red ribbon around would not have carried more authority than this statement. Mr. Walley, Sophy and I stood on the bank by the lock gates and saw on their far side in the very center of the channel a little trickle of water that would scarcely have floated a child's paper boat. As water gypsies we were washed up.

The lockkeeper had a telephone and also a friend in Llangollen who owned a car. Within an hour the friend had arrived as close to the canal as he could drive. A wide meadow intervened. Sophy and I plodded across this, Mr. Walley carrying the two bags we had packed. It was an ignominious exit. There was not even the drama of a ship-wreck to remove us. We were promised the water would certainly come by the following morning. Mr. Walley would await its arrival and bring the *Venturer* on to Llangollen.

We rode in an ancient rattling automobile, but the drive of perhaps fifteen miles was through a magnificent countryside of green hills, woods and the exuberant River Dee that wanders noisily through this landscape. The road winds too, and I am at best a nervous motorist. Eight days of travel on foot or at a maximum boat speed of four miles an hour convinced me our ancient taxi was traveling like a meteor. When I shrilled this conviction to the driver, he was indignant. He showed me the speedometer registered a little over thirty miles an hour. I was convinced then the speedometer was as broken down and as full of lumps as the upholstery on which I bounced. I persuaded the chauffeur to slow down to a little over twenty and even then felt apprehensive and uncomfortable. The wind roaring past my ears and my eyes streaming, I remembered suddenly the things Grandmother Kimbrough had said after her baptismal ride in Grandfather's first automobile and wished I had been more sympathetic. I was distracted however, and considerably reconciled to my situation, when the driver identified a landmark that came into view as we careened, I thought, around a curve and came mercifully into an open stretch. "That's the Pontcysyllte Aqueduct," he said. "It's a hundred and twenty feet above the river. It's made of cast iron and it's over a thousand feet long. It carries the canal. It's Telford's work and you'd of come along it had the water been proper."

The aqueduct we had traveled was earthbound compared to this. I stared up at the thing in horror and murmured a prayer of gratitude. I promised that never again would I ask for rain and deplore a drought. That beautiful dry canal bed had been a merciful obstacle put up across my path to save me from traveling a hundred and twenty feet above a roaring river on a thread of water held up by jack straws even if they were made of cast iron.

Simultaneously with the recognition that Pauline in her Perils had not been bound to a trestle more inexorably than I, nor rescued from it more fortuitously, I realized my rescue might turn out to be a double feature. If the water could be held back just a little longer I not only

138

would have escaped the viaduct, I would not have to go through the tunnel beyond Llangollen, that other thrilling adventure mapper Sophy had offered me as one of the inducements to this trip. Musing happily over one delivery and the possibility of another I permitted our driver a spurt to thirty that brought us with a flourish to the door of the Bridge End Hotel on the banks of the River Dee in Llangollen.

CHAPTER ELEVEN

W E STAYED two days and nights in Llangollen. The natural setting of the town is enchanting, but alas it has become crowded with souvenir shops and busloads of tourists to buy these wares. We found the hotel comfortable with good food. We took walking trips in the neighborhood to Llantysilio and Rhewl. We did not walk over the mountains nor ascend Moel Gamelyn. We wanted to be able to touch base frequently in the hope of a message, or even the arrival of Mr. Walley on the *Venturer*. Someday I shall go back, I hope, in order to explore the surrounding country, see Chirk Castle, the seat of the Myddelton family, walk in the mountains, visit the monastic ruins of Valle Crucis and those of Crow Castle. Early July is the time of the Musical Eisteddfod, the Welsh festival of music and poetry at Llangollen that brings folk dancers in their national dress from Scandinavia, Central Europe, Italy, Spain, and more.

Although it was tantalizing to be in the neighborhood and yet not be able to take long excursions, we counted one place alone well worth the visit to Llangollen. This is Plas Newydd, a small estate that now belongs to the City

Council and is open to the public. From 1780 to 1831 it was the residence of Lady Eleanor Butler and Miss Sarah Ponsonby. Even the indifferent and speedy sightseer who checks off on his itinerary the places he has "done" must be piqued to further exploring and reading when he has once heard the story of these extraordinary women.

They were members of two of the foremost families in Ireland. They became friends at boarding school and returning to their respective homes were bitterly unhappy. Each was being pressed to a marriage for money, though even the families admitted the individuals selected were distasteful. The two miserable young women corresponded with each other and through this medium developed a plan they carried out.

On a night in May in 1778 these unhappy and courageous friends left home and family and together made their way into Wales and eventually to Llangollen. Certainly neither of them had ever before so much as gone shopping unaccompanied. How they came to choose let alone reach Llangollen, part of the trip by sailboat, I have not been able to discover, but the story of the fifty years there is almost as extraordinary as their flight.

From the day they moved into the house they had been able to acquire, Plas Newydd and twelve acres of land surrounding it, they never again spent a night away. They traveled widely about the countryside, occasionally leaving before daybreak for a visit to friends but always returning by dawn of the following day without having passed a night in a house other than their own. Though such daring independence had created a scandal of a magnitude that befitted their rank, people visited them. Not because they were objects of curiosity, but because they were two intelligent, lively women who read widely, spoke wittily and kept in touch through their reading and their monumental correspondence with people and events in the world. The little village they had chosen happened to be on the stagecoach road between London and Dublin. Travelers passing through stopped off to visit them and to see the beautiful gardens that over the years they created and developed. Had Lady Eleanor and Miss Ponsonby kept a guestbook it would contain the signatures of the most distinguished people of their time: Sir Walter Scott, Wordsworth, the Duke of Wellington; it is an astonishing list. But these names are included casually in Lady Eleanor's diary among such events of the day as the birth of a calf to their beloved cow, or the discharging of a maid for "idleness, dirt and *such a tongue.*" The entries are of their other friends too, the villagers, who brought their troubles, recorded in the journal with tender concern.

Of all the *souvenirs de voyage* I have ever seen, this house contains the most improbable collection. The Ladies fancied carved oak and there is very little space outside or in that is free of it. This ornate forest grew by means of gifts brought by the visiting travelers. I myself follow the custom of bringing a house present to the hostess whose house I am visiting, but my present is of a size that takes up little room in an average bag. I do not arrive dragging behind me in some fashion a carved oaken beam and I do not understand how travelers of that day in whatever form of conveyance they used, managed to lug along with them, or even have sent—and by what means?—carved oak. Not the size of a paper cutter but of a size to panel a room or a

section of the exterior of the house. It is all there to be seen now.

The topiary and a good part of the garden are still preserved. The town itself is full of souvenirs of their Ladies. A silhouette made of them during their lifetime is reproduced on post cards, ashtrays and the like. The silhouette itself shows them to have been not very tall, plump, and dressed in eighteenth-century riding habits including the hat; a costume they invariably wore indoors and out, daytime and evening.

Chief Justice Charles Kendall Bushe wrote of them in 1805 in a letter to his wife after a call on "The Ladies." "They gave me all the news of Dublin, London, Cheltenham, Paris and everywhere in a moment; everything they said was pointed, naïve, polished and interesting—sometimes satirical, always witty."

The Ladies were cordial to visitors who were either known to them or came with proper letters of introduction. They were high-handed with tourists. An entry in Lady Eleanor's journal of June 14th, 1789, reads: "Peter the Smith, came to say that some company were coming to see the garden. We sent to inform them no person was admitted to see the shrubbery who did not send their names in, but if they would acquaint us with theirs they should be welcome to see it. They declined to do this and consequently went away with their curiosity ungratified."

Lady Eleanor died in 1829, Miss Ponsonby in 1831.

We spent Saturday and Sunday nights at the Bridge End Hotel. (The official guide to Llangollen includes in its list of accommodations "Temperance and Private hotels." I

144

doubt I would make one of these my selection on a subsequent visit.) During this time we did not see the *Venturer* nor have word from Mr. Walley. On Monday morning the weather changed. Rain came and a telephone call from Mr. Walley. He could not reach us on the boat, but he had got turned around and was back at Ellesmere. Sophy and I held a sad conference and brief, because Mr. Walley waited at the other end of the wire.

Our decision was to drive to Ellesmere, gather up our belongings left on the boat, and return by train to London. Mr. Walley would deliver the boat to Stone. We reminded him to leave there Miss Ritchie's lantern and guidebook. This weather was anything but ideal for cruising. We had had beautiful, sunny, warm days; better leave at the peak and not taper off into sodden discomfort. We drove in a taxi to Ellesmere, arriving there in something less than an hour and covering more than the distance of Friday's and half of Saturday's trip on the boat. While the car waited we packed and said good-by to Mr. Walley, but only a temporary farewell. He had promised to be our captain for the big cruise when we would be five, setting out from Stone again on another vessel, the *Maid Marysue,* a larger crew but Captain Walley at the tiller.

CHAPTER TWELVE

ON SATURDAY the 15th of June, Sophy, Dorothy and Howard Lindsay and Arthur Kober left Euston Station. One member of the crew was missing. The cook, the galley slave, E. Kimbrough was abed at Madame Pandit's, victim of the Asian flu. I had boasted as I sat beside her sickbed I never caught anything. Sophy and I had been dismayed on our return from our cruise to find her still with fever and confined to bed though she protested by comparison with her previous misery she was entirely well. Feeling guilty because we had had such a good time and she such a poor one, each of us had spent as much time as she would permit in the sickroom. And each time she expressed an apprehension that our presence made us susceptible to this wretched plague Sophy and I outdid each other in a boast of our invulnerability to germs.

Sophy vindicated her boasting but on the 13th of June when Madame Pandit was recovered and we were with her at the "Trooping the Colour" in celebration of the Queen's official birthday I was invaded by a violent chill. I have never been hit so unexpectedly and with such impact, nor, I might add in such an unhandy place as the center of a grandstand filled to an overflow of four or five rows of standees. There was no possible way of getting out and so I chattered and shook while the Queen inspected her troops and bands played. Once I was home however, I was there to stay, by the doctor's orders. Since the time I had the measles and could not go to the circus I have not been so ragingly filled with a sense of injustice and frustration as on the Saturday morning I glowered from my bed at Sophy waving good-by from the doorway of my room.

I caught up with them the following Wednesday the 19th at Rugby. They had got in, they said, only a few minutes before I arrived around half past five at the Grand Hotel. There were two more arrivals within the next hour.

Someone on *Life* magazine had seen a paragraph in *Variety* that the Howard Lindsays and Arthur Kober were going to travel the canals of England. From such little statements pages of pictures grow. *Life*'s New York office cabled its London branch to find those travelers and secure permission to join us for two days or so, snapping and note-taking all the way. I was the one the London office had found! The others were already on a canal. I had telephoned from London because I had their itinerary and waved it threateningly every morning when the doctor visited me. I had their acceptance of the visitors from *Life* and within an hour of my arrival in Rugby they were with us. Miss Lynam and Mr. Burrows. They turned out to be, both of them, young, pleasant and considerate.

At cocktails together in the Grand Hotel we learned they had rented a boat with a captain and would be on it ready to follow us at whatever hour we planned to take off in the morning. "Not later than nine-fifteen," Howard said, and I very nearly dropped my glass of white wine and soda. Sophy saw my convulsion of surprise and murmured in a low tone to me, "You never saw such a change, wait till I tell you."

I had to wait until we had gone up at about ten o'clock to the room we shared. The *Life* contingent had left after cocktails. They were staying a few miles away. The original five of us had dined at the hotel and all during the meal I had prodded them with questions, needlessly, because they were in a fever to tell me what had happened, and how they'd loved every minute of it. But it was only when Sophy and I were alone I was able to pick up a clear thread from the very start at Euston Station.

Sophy had been in a dither that day, she admitted. On her way to the station she had almost wanted to escape the whole trip and in the taxi had worked herself into a rage at me for getting ill. The trip had been my idea in the beginning and the crew were closer friends of mine than of hers. Although she thought them delightful she felt shy with them. She knew how uneasy they were about this expedition, totally unlike anything any of the three had done before. She had realized, too, she must run the trip and make it palatable all by herself. By the time she had joined them on the station platform, she said, she would have been happy not to see them or me as long as she lived.

The picture and her frame of mind had changed almost at the moment of entering the railway carriage. Arthur Kober had hung up his topcoat on a hook behind him and had then sat down on the tail of the coat, wrenching it

148

from the hook and tearing the tab by which it had been suspended. Sophy had immediately volunteered to sew it back in place. I interrupted at this point of her recital with as sharp an astonishment as I had experienced at Howard's announcement that we would leave at 9:15 A.M.

The only time I had ever seen Sophy wield a needle had been a great many years ago when she had accompanied me on a visit to my grandparents in Muncie, Indiana, and during that visit had sewn on a button in the presence of my grandmother. It had been a flagrant showing off on Sophy's part and the only thing it had shown off to my grandmother was Sophy's unfamiliarity with a needle and thread. Sophy had attached the button, and the garment to which it was her intention to affix it, to the skirt she was wearing, the underclothing beneath it, and a portion of her thigh wielding the needle the while in a fashion I had hitherto seen employed only by Normandy fishermen while mending their nets. Grandmother had approached Sophy with a pair of scissors and having separated Sophy's person from her sewing had taken over.

Sophy was impatient with this reminiscence. She had done a little sewing since those days she insisted. Anyway she had impressed Arthur, made him grateful and she herself had from that moment on felt cozy.

Dorothy had begun to smile, Sophy said, the moment they boarded the train, and had not left off enjoying everything as it came. Sophy had been a little dismayed by the amount of Dorothy's luggage, but she had explained most of it was made up of little bags she intended to take care of herself, and Sophy said she did. By the time she had them distributed about her person she looked and walked in a manner faintly reminiscent of the man in the circus who balances and sustains members of his family on hips, shoulders and head and then moves about with this encumbrance.

Their marketing in Stone had been quickly accomplished, Sophy said pointedly. They had not looked for an ice bucket nor any other outlandish thing. Therefore, they had had time in the afternoon to hire a car and drive to Ingestre Hall, the "Historic Home of the Earle of Shrewsbury," its guidebook says. The house is Jacobean, built in 1613 of rose brick. The church was designed by Christopher Wren. I have Sophy's assurance the house, the church, the gardens belong on a tourist's list of "musts." She was equally positive about the difficulty of coaxing Arthur and Howard from their delighted inspection of the collection in the coach house. In addition to broughams, phaetons and wagonettes there is the State Coach, more accurately called the "Dress Chariot." It was last used to carry the present Earl and Countess of Shrewsbury to the coronation of Queen Elizabeth II.

They had begun the big adventure on the *Maid Marysue* at noon on Sunday but, Sophy said, they were not wished godspeed by the local press as we had been. Evidently Americans on a canal no longer made news. The first day's run had been short by plan and so they were able even with the late start to include a time ashore to see Shugborough, that Sophy and I had visited. This time, arriving within the hours of admission, they had been able to visit the interior. Handsome, she said, but not more beautiful than the field of buttercups, nor so dramatic as the

150

avenue of rhododendrons. They had seen no lovers in the
hedgerows.

They had spent the night at the Eaton Lodge Country
Club at Rugeley. Though their accommodations had been
comfortable they were dismayed to find on arrival that on
Sunday the meal of the day was at noon and the evening
provisions cold and scanty. Sophy said she had felt a return
of panic as group leader, but discovered that though
hungry her group was happy. The next day they had got
under way at eleven, had a beautiful run, the day warm and
sunny, the countryside beautiful, and had reached Lichfield around five in the afternoon. Sophy and Dorothy
moaned, she said, as they walked the streets of the town
that I was not there. This is where Samuel Johnson was
born and where for many years he returned annually. His
house can be visited and is now a museum of Johnsoniana.
There is a statue of Boswell in the marketplace. The Cathedral of St. Mary and St. Chad completed in 1325 delighted
them of course. They wandered about the close, visited the
church of St. Chad that also dates back to the thirteenth
century, and after dinner at the George Hotel they had
walked again. Sophy told me she and Dorothy had sat
until late watching the lights go out one by one in the
lovely houses around the green and almost tiptoed back to
the hotel not wanting to break the hush and spell of another century that hung heavy over the town at night.

The following morning Sophy had received a shock
that had rocked her. Coming down for breakfast at about
half past eight she had found Howard already there. When
she had asked anxiously if he were ill and had been unable
to sleep, he had answered crisply he had never felt better

and was only eager to get under way. He was impatient of
dawdling. This declaration had stunned Sophy to speech-
lessness. Though I questioned such an assertion, she reiterated she had been unable to find a word to answer, and
was still dumb when Dorothy and Arthur had come nimbly
into the dining room and at sight of Sophy queried, "How
soon do you think we can start?"

They had been under way at ten o'clock, had another
beautiful day and come to Nuneaton in Warwickshire for
the night at the Newdegate Arms Hotel. Another day's run
beautiful and serene had brought them to the Grand Hotel
at Rugby and at last I had caught up with them.

We did not leave Rugby so early on Thursday morning
as Howard had wished, but the delay was not because of
dalliance. We were down at breakfast a little after eight. At
the moment of entering the dining room I was introduced
to an already established custom of the crew. Sophy and
I had come downstairs together chatting amicably, but as
I was heading toward a table at which I saw Howard and
Arthur, she stopped me peremptorily and lowered her
voice to a whisper.

"The men eat breakfast alone," she said, "and don't
speak to us until they have had their coffee."

We skirted widely around their area and took a table
at some distance from theirs. When we were seated well out
of range Sophy continued her explanation. "There was so
much to tell you last night," she said, "I forgot about this."
She told me they had started out eating breakfast together
and the men were very polite, so polite in fact she could see
they were under a strain. It occurred to her they were used
to breakfasting alone and Dorothy had confirmed it about

152

Vasiliu

Howard. Thereupon she had suggested they separate for this meal and the two men had capered with pleasure and gratitude. She had added to this indulgence by going out early and getting newspapers. "The dear optimists," she said, "thought they would find a stack of newspapers at the cigarette stands, but there is neither a cigarette stand nor newspapers in an English inn. Dorothy thinks I'm going too far. She says I'm making it hard for her when she and Howard get home, but wait till you see how jolly they are after breakfast with paper; fairly wreathed in smiles, and you notice they don't speak to each other."

I allowed myself a timid glance in their direction. Sure enough there was no sound from their table. Each was concealed from the other behind his journal and neither giving a look in our direction.

As I watched them in their happy isolation Dorothy came into the room, paused a moment at the threshold and spotting Sophy and me followed much the same detour we had taken. Reaching us she said in a low tone scarcely above a whisper, "Good morning, dears. They seem very happy."

"They are," Sophy assured her. "They haven't looked up once." I keyed my voice to the pitch Sophy and Dorothy had sounded and we chatted happily but with conscientious restraint.

We were interrupted by a hearty "Hello there, hello! Good morning, how is everybody?"

Howard and Arthur had risen from their table and were approaching us each with a newspaper folded under his arm. They were smiling, their eyes were bright, their step jaunty, their gay greetings kaleidoscoping into a genial confusion of well-being and gladsome anticipation of the day in our company. They urged us not to hurry through our meal but enjoy it, Howard adding it would perhaps be a good idea to get started as soon as possible. It was not difficult to sort out from these contradictory statements the suggestion they hoped we would follow. We finished our meal quickly.

Shopping was first on the day's schedule I was told, and this brought no surprise to me. It was the order Sophy and I had followed, but now I learned we shopped only for lunch. Breakfast and dinner were always at an inn. Nevertheless, incidentals for elevenses and tea must be included. These occasions were as dutifully observed as I had catered to them on the *Venturer*.

Rugby is itself pleasant. We first explored the famous school, then shopped deviously, following an enticing lane off the main street, circling to the thoroughfare again only to see another that provoked investigation.

When we finally came back to the hotel we found a representative of the Waterways with his own car and a taxi besides to take us to Brinklow where the boat was tied. As we were stowing our bags, provisions, etc., he suggested we might like to go by way of Coventry, so near it would seem a pity to pass it by.

We said to one another afterward, "Never pass by any suggestion that is made of something to see. Let nine of these be without particular interest if the tenth is Coventry."

Of course we knew of the hideous damage done to Coventry by the bombing. All of us had read of the dreadful night on the 14th of November, 1940, worse than all the others, that very nearly wiped away the place and the people in it. What we had not known was that city authorities, with a sensitive perceptiveness for which all visitors must be forever grateful, had decreed the Cathedral be left in the proud dignity of its wounds and scars. The noble framework stands naked, allowing no one to leave that spot with such a palliative as "One would never know there had been such destruction." There is no roof, there is no glass in the windows. Nothing obstructs the view through their frames of the green country around and off to one side at some distance the new cathedral in construction.

Niches along the sidewalls still carry the identifying inscriptions, cut in stone, that marked the particular altar of each guild. Stone does not burn nor melt and twist as the girders had twisted into shapeless oblivion. Where the floor had been, and later a mass of rubble, was now fresh, green young grass that brought a look of innocence, like a baby's blanket in that gray, gaunt crib. The blanket went all the way from the entrance to the foot of what had been the altar. That place is marked now by a tall cross shaped from charred timbers and inscribed with the words "Father Forgive."

After a while, when the impact of the place had dulled a bit, I took some pictures. I saw Sophy at some distance from me. Her back was turned, she was looking through one of the window frames. I joined her to ask advice about setting my lens in this bright sunlight on dark stone. She was not setting her camera at anything. I doubt she was focusing on the view through the empty window. Tears were sliding down her face and her hands holding a camera were shaking.

We reached the *Maid Marysue* at Brinklow about half

past twelve. The young people from *Life* were waiting for us in their own boat, a cruiser smaller than ours. I scarcely paused to say "hello" in my eagerness to investigate our own vessel but even more to see Mr. Walley. Within a second of disgracing myself I remembered my watchword for the American in England. "Restraint." At the moment Mr. Walley came into view from a cabin I checked my leap toward him much in the manner I had seen blue herons pulling back to make a landing. I advanced with sedate cordiality. There is something to be said in favor of sedate cordiality. Mr. Walley was convincing and heartwarming and he inquired about my health by hoping I was myself again. I translated this as an assertion that no one else could have taken my place. I was only a little disconcerted when he assured me on my solicitous query his tea and elevenses had been altogether "proper."

To my surprise I discovered we had become so stylish on this trip as to have an assistant captain. I was introduced to Mr. Fitter, a slim dark-haired tanned young man who provoked an immediate distrust in me by being extremely cordial. While Mr. Walley stowed the bags and provisions he showed me the *Maid Marysue.* She was not so picturesque as the *Venturer,* but an attractive motor cruiser. She had been delivered to Stone from the base of the "Maid Line" at Thames Ditton. She differed from the boats they provide for cruising on the Thames, in width. Canal travel requires narrower breadth. I found there were two cabins forward, each with an upper and lower bunk on one side of a narrow aisle. A tall cupboard stood opposite the bunks. There were windows at the level of the upper berth. The boat was run from the center at an open space that divided the cruiser in half. Directly in front of this one spot on the ship that would never be unoccupied, while the boat was running, was the lavatory. To reach it, it was necessary to duck under and around the helmsman, who stood on a low platform in order to allow him to see over the roof. Ship designers must possess in common a stunning ingenuity to work out the most unlikely spot for the one place on the boat a passenger would like to visit inconspicuously.

Aft of the engines and wheel was one large and comfortable cabin. A broad bench across the stern could be a bed at night. A thick, upholstered cushion covered the seat and a great many small pillows formed a back. A similar couch, though narrower, was along one side. There were in addition several chairs, a stove, sink, and under the sink a sizable cupboard for supplies. It was a pleasant room but I discovered was used infrequently.

As soon as we were all aboard and under way I was introduced to the pattern of the day, and there was nothing haphazard about it. The two men went immediately into the nearer of the two forward cabins. They did not go together and I feel reasonably sure the order of precedence had also been definitely established. Each came out dressed in his yachting outfit, soft shirt, slacks, rubber-soled shoes and cap with a visor. Dorothy, Sophy and I, as we waited in the main cabin, put away in the cupboard the supplies we had purchased. When the men were dressed, they climbed immediately over the side in the center to a narrow ledge and from this to the roof over the forward cabins, where they settled themselves. Sophy, Dorothy and I in turn moved to the farther of the two fore cabins and changed to our boating outfits, blouse and slacks for Sophy and me, blouse, skirt for Dorothy, rubber-soled shoes for each of us, dark glasses, no hat. We followed the men to the roof and I found the pattern included Mr. Fitter's placing there a great many cushions from the cabins. These could be piled to make a backrest or spread out like a mattress on which to lie.

Within a very short time too, I was aware that for my watchword of restraint Dorothy had substituted watchfulness and flexibility. She watched for sun, shade or breeze and adjusted her costume accordingly. Her luggage for all its number of pieces had not included, she admitted, provision for warm weather because everyone had told her to prepare for dampness and cold. Neither of these two prophecies had been realized. The sun was bright and hot. There was a breeze, but it was wayward. Dorothy followed each of its caprices. To remedy her deficiency in costume she had purchased soon after the beginning of the cruise a sun top, the only one she told me, apologetically, she could find. It was a dainty confection, but not one I think she would have chosen from a wide selection. This was of nylon disguised as chiffon, strapless, shirred in narrow rows, and of the shade of pink to match the inside of a watermelon. Used as a distress signal at the end of a pole it would have drawn attention from a considerable area.

With this she brought to the roof a sweater and a little pouch she opened as soon as she had arranged herself on the cushions. It disgorged cold cream and sun-tan lotion. When the breeze was not with us she slipped from blouse to bodice in a presto-chango she must have learned from Mr. Thurston and with a modest concealment a Quaker could have endorsed. This accomplished she applied the sun-tan lotion. When the breeze returned, she was the first to mark its coming. The blouse replaced the bodice and though she did not wet her finger and then point it in the air, she seemed to know instantly both the strength and direction of wind. By her judgment of these she decided for

or against a sweater as a top layer. Sometimes she shifted within a minute her judgment that a sweater had been necessary, and with equal frequency she returned to the original sun top. This gave her very little time for shifting from cold cream as an avoidance of wind burn to sun lotion for tanning, but it gave her exercise the rest of us could not even approximate.

To follow Dorothy's change of temperature I could not allow myself to be distracted for more than a quick glance at the landscape, beautiful as it was. Therefore I did not see Sophy leave us and knew she had gone only when we heard her halloo that lunch was ready. I was dismayed I had not gone down to help her. Furthermore I was discomfited at having been replaced. I had considered operation of the galley my prerogative and my insistence on approbation and commiseration had enriched my enjoyment of the position. I was now without portfolio just a member of the crew, and I was not happy with such anonymity.

A table in the main cabin had been let down from the wall and covered with a gay cloth. We ate cold ham, fresh crusty bread still warm, salad, cheese and, miracle of miracles, there was iced tea for me. A tall glass of it with lemon, that is more merciful to me than to Mr. Walley, and actual ice. I even poked the lovely cubes to make sure they were real. Dorothy, I found, had provided the miracle by way of Hammacher Schlemmer. I was shown the invention from which it came—a fairly large plump square of pale green that looked not unlike a rubber pillow open at one end. Whatever the material actually was, its magic property was refrigeration. Placed in an icebox overnight it would keep at icebox temperature for the whole of the following day, whatever was placed inside it. I asked if innkeepers had not been surprised by a request to put this object in their cold storage; it was quite a variation from the more conventional request to lock up a guest's valuables in the safe. Dorothy insisted each proprietor had been more interested than surprised and I conceded this to be par for a British course. The existence of ice and the landlord's willingness to share it, however, seemed to me supernatural. I learned too the invention was now a storage place for our milk and butter and commended the thrift this permitted since the milk would not go sour and have to be thrown out.

The men requested beer and Sophy groaned. Every day the same thing happened, she said. She would think she had got from the cupboard, before the table went down, everything that would be needed, but invariably she forgot something. She refused our offers of assistance; not one of us she affirmed had had the daily practice required to crawl under the table, open the cupboard door from that position, extract what had been forgotten, and back out again without a crack on the head or an upheaval of the dining table.

She was just backing out on all fours when a voice calling "Hello everybody" startled everyone but caused her to rap her head smartly on the table's edge, tilting it precariously. Our visitors were Miss Lynam and Mr. Burrows. They had come aboard bringing their own lunch. Sophy hastily on her feet started what sounded like an offer of beer, but it trailed away before it reached definitiveness. She muttered to me instead, "Not when that young man's got a camera in his hand will I go under the table." She need not have taken such precautions. She might just as well have gone to ground again. The pictures that appeared in *Life* included a splendid reproduction of Sophy emerging from beneath the table, taken from the rear.

The minute we had finished eating Sophy said she and I would return to the roof. It was not so much a suggestion as a listing under "order of the day." When I demurred, murmuring something about washing up, Dorothy spoke authoritatively, though she is always gentle.

"We worked it all out the first day," she explained. "It's much easier to work alone in the cabin. When there are two they get in each other's way, so Sophy fixes lunch and I clean up. I like doing that, but it bothers me to have someone else around."

"Except us," Arthur put in, and I saw that he and Howard were still at the table. "We play gin," Arthur explained, "while the little woman works. This adds zest, makes us feel very masculine in a medieval way. Sometimes one of us cracks a whip."

Dorothy eyeing him speculatively inquired, "Would you like to empty the garbage, Arthur?"

I think he blanched; I know he winced. "I'll have to send for my analyst," he said.

"At the rate you're winning from me," Howard told him, "it won't cost you a nickel."

I stopped at the engine room, if that is the name for the space in the center from which the boat was run, to chat with Mr. Walley. Mr. Fitter was at the tiller. Because of our late start we had not tied up for lunch. The two captains had eaten in shifts, but both had now finished. Mr. Walley asked if I had been watching the photographer. I admitted I had not, but forebore to explain my absorption in Dorothy's sleight of hand had focused my complete attention.

"Goes over the ground like a galloping hostrich," Mr.

Walley assured me. "Never saw the like of it. Aye, and with all the packs he carries joomps about like a mountain goat."

I went to the roof very soon, impatient to see for myself the offspring of such remarkably blended antecedents. Sophy was stretched out on a length of pillows, but this

did not make a good observation post I decided. After a few moments' experimenting I devised one that from then on was not only accredited but allotted to me. I discovered a hatch over the cabin farthest forward. It was possible to come and go by this opening instead of having to squeeze round the cramped center section and the two pilots. Better even than this convenience, however, was that when opened it provided a well into which to swing feet and legs while sitting on the cushions at the rim. At the call of "Bridge ahead," I later discovered, I could bend over and down holding on to either side. Head almost between my knees I was exposed scarcely above deck level. No matter how often I was told it was an exaggerated precaution, I made this obeisance. Coming close to every bridge on every canal we traveled, I had a horrid expectation the boat alone would scarcely go under; anything on it would be scraped off. The first morning I used my discovered hatch as egress from our dressing room, I had an unexpected encounter. My head came up through the hatch and face to face with an inquisitive cow. The boat was still tied to the bank and the creature had come to investigate. As I pushed the hatch open, she had stretched her neck over it.

There are two discomforts on canal boats of both types we employed. Apart from the location of the lavatory I count one other; a remarkably small total, yet I cannot call it an accomplishment of designers in a nation that eschews comfort. The second discomfort is a lack of open deck space fore or aft where chairs could be placed. The length of the boat is given to cabins. The engine and navigator occupy the only open space. Though this area includes a bench it is not a pleasant place to sit because of the noise from the engine. Therefore to be outdoors one must occupy the roof. A flat space with no difference in level to allow bending the knees can be agonizing to the muscles. Sitting for any length of time with the legs straight out can bring about a loss of power of locomotion, and pain as well when one tries to stand. Legs crossed tailor fashion will produce much the same effect. Lying at full length

makes possible an uninterrupted view of the sky but not much else. Therefore I list myself among the discoverers of new lands, rivers and stars, by reason of my finding a hole into which to swing my legs while sitting up.

The descendant of mountain goat and ostrich justified Mr. Walley's appraisal of photographer Burrows' genealogy. I located him in action as we came from under a bridge and I brought my head up from the hatch. Mr. Burrows was standing on top of the bridge and, camera between his hands, was bending forward at a preposterous angle, yet he did not fall on us. Before he was fully straightened upright he was leaping, camera in hand, and it was anything but pocket-size, knapsack over one shoulder, another sort of pouch over the other. I had not realized until I saw them move what long legs he had, and when they were in motion I could not see them clearly because they drove so fast, operating like piston rods. They carried him down the side of the bridge onto the towpath abreast of us and beyond almost before in Sophy's phraseology you could say "knife." I was facing the stern and by the time I had turned around to watch he was ahead of the boat and I then saw we were coming to a lock. By the time we had reached it Mr. Burrows was on it; actually balancing on the narrow gate, his equipment still with him, swinging. Camera to one eye he snapped again and again as we came closer. He only left it in a few bounds when Mr. Walley approached with the windlass.

No packages on a Christmas day in my childhood produced the number of surprises by which I was jolted on this first half day. They started even before Gypsy Rose Stickney turned dishwasher, but reached a climax when I saw

168

Howard and Arthur bolt from the cabin, leap ashore and join Mr. Walley at the lock while Sophy remained lolling on her cushions. I had supposed she would take the tiller and Mr. Fitter would go ashore with Mr. Walley. Mr. Fitter stood at the tiller. I was shaken to see Arthur, when the gates began to open, leap the breach with a nimbleness that made him first cousin to Mr. Burrows and a mountain goat. He took his place at the gate on the opposite side, and helped open it. When Mr. Walley had gone on to the further gate and we had moved into the lock, Arthur and Howard, these two dreamers from the theater that makes them not like other folk, closed the gates behind us and dropped the paddles. They then moved forward to help Mr. Walley complete the other operation and, boarding the boat with him, returned to their game of gin.

Dorothy joined Sophy and me on the roof soon after we had left the lock and a little later the men came on top. Howard was cheerfully resigned, he said, and Arthur apologetic. Howard explained that Arthur won every game. Arthur emphasized he had been told before leaving to watch out for Lindsay because he could clean up anyone at that game; therefore, Arthur insisted ambiguously, he was playing better than he really could because he was "watching out," whereas Howard was having bad luck. Howard denied his skill and corroborated the bad luck. The only time in recent months he had won, he said, he had not even been permitted to put a hand on his winnings. The loser, a newcomer at the Players Club the evening of the game, had made the common mistake of transposing Howard's identity with his playwriting collaborator's and sent the check to Russel Crouse.

Arthur went to the aft roof with cushions and a book. Howard at my invitation tried my discovery and finding there was room in the well for him made himself comfortable against pillows at its rim. We watched a soft landscape slowly unroll before us, and listened to birds singing. The water smacked the banks, and the reeds along them bowed and crackled faintly as they touched one another. Ashore we had animated conversation, but here we all spoke very little. I asked Howard if the cruise had been as he had anticipated it, and he said:

"In the beginning—perhaps the first day and a half—I was restless. I was still geared to a pace all of us keep at home. My feeling was if we're going to Lichfield, or whatever, let's get there. Now my feeling is, why do we want to go to Lichfield? Why leave this boat? I can't remember having such a sense of tranquillity and contentment as I have now. Every night I'm sorry to leave the canal and in the morning I can hardly wait to get back to it and away from the town, however charming it has been."

A little while after that he added and must have been thinking about it in the meantime:

"When I get home I wonder how I can convey what this trip does. You can't say the beautiful country is responsible; after all there's lots of beautiful country. You can't say it's being on a boat. I don't know how I'm going to tell them that it has to do with a slow boat on a narrow channel so still the water doesn't even ripple, and so narrow you feel you're floating through meadows and up and down hills."

I asked if he had any special people in mind to whom he wanted to describe our cruise. He said he'd been having some fun with that idea, sorting out among his friends the ones he thought might like to do this, applying the cruise as a kind of yardstick to their temperaments. Sophy overheard this, and began a speculation aloud about a mutual friend. It was the beginning of an absorbing game to which we reverted time and again during the trip.

Around four o'clock I suggested somewhat belligerently I might be permitted to make tea. Once more I was demoted by Sophy's information that Mr. Fitter took care of tea as well as morning elevenses. Arthur joined us. When Mr. Fitter had removed the cups and was washing up in the galley—such luxury making me a little giddy, I said— we left the boat to walk along the towpath. Mr. Burrows was still leaping and snapping and took several shots of us, proving as we advanced toward him he could run backward almost as fast as forward, and without any more caution than he displayed on the gate of a lock. Miss Lynam had remained on their boat, and it stayed ahead of us in order, I suppose, not to be included in any of the pictures. She had been taking notes, I think, of what Mr. Burrows was photographing, but seeing us she jumped ashore and joined the promenade. We had discovered a very pleasant place for stretching was along a lock. The boat was nosed in then toward the bank allowing those who would operate the gates to jump ashore. We would then be picked up on the other side. If there were a series, or the locks not too widely apart, we would continue along the towpath to the next one. There was no danger this time of running aground when we nosed in, if one were reasonably careful. The canals were at normal level now and Mr. Walley was always careful.

We came into Braunston about half past five but long before that Mr. Walley had pointed out the spire of its church that is a landmark for miles around. We tied up at what Mr. Walley would have called a "proper dock" and were welcomed by Mr. Finnigan of the waterways and an assistant, each with a car. A path from dock to the road was so narrow we traveled single file passing some wooden sheds. Dorothy always makes polite conversation after an introduction, partly because of an inherent friendliness and unmistakably a consequence of meticulous childhood training in manners. And so while the rest of us plodded along the path silently I heard Dorothy ahead of me inquire of Mr. Finnigan the purpose of these sheds, though I'm sure she had not the slightest interest in them. "Is it a boatworks?" she asked. Mr. Finnigan, just ahead of her, not pausing but turning his head said casually over his shoulder, "Oh yes, but it's also where they paint the tinware for the barge people. It's a very old craft, and this is the only place along the canals I know of where it's done."

I thought Dorothy would fall down. She reeled, spun around and very nearly crashed into me. Pointing to the sheds with a shaking hand she gabbled.

"I know, I know," I told her, "I heard him." Had I not I would not have known what my dear friend was endeavoring to convey because she was in such a tremor of excitement. I didn't blame her. Dorothy and I at the word "antiques" stiffen like pointers to a huntsman's horn but a mention of anything early and Victorian dissolves her into a kind of ague. Accurately these utensils on the narrow boat predate the Victorian; nevertheless they have a family resemblance. Dorothy had heard about them at the outset

172

of this trip. She had even seen one or two on commercial barges they had passed, but she had been told they were impossible to find today nor would any barge woman relinquish hers for whatever price.

Dorothy and I started back on the run. We knew the entrance must be at the dock. Howard and Arthur were behind us. They were ninepins to our assault. Mr. Finnigan retraced his steps, but Sophy, who had led off, was not aware of the commotion behind and no one thought to tell her. She reached the road before she discovered no one was with her and by the time she found us she was a little testy. One look at the objects displayed to us and she was pacified. There they were set in a line on a bench, not many of them, but just like the ones about which we had read and of which we'd had glimpses on passing barges; teapots, water cans and a vessel with broad bottom and short handle for scooping up water. All of them were painted in the traditional pattern of roses, bright yellow, red and pink on a background of green. The craftsman who painted them was a handsome old man. He would not have sold us his pieces had Mr. Walley not been there. But because Mr. Walley came of barge people and we were with him the transaction was permitted. I could not picture a place for them in my New York apartment, but Dorothy knew these things belonged in the Lindsays' house in the country and Howard was very nearly as enthusiastic as she. Sophy and I with Arthur's assistance managed to secrete a water dipper. A vessel that is more than a foot in diameter is not easily concealed, but the three of us remained in close formation. The inspiration had been Sophy's. She had first coaxed us out of the shed by asking us to help her with something on the boat and once out of hearing told us she had overheard Howard say ruefully that day to Dorothy he felt very badly he had nothing for her birthday tomorrow. Sophy had meant to pass this on to us in the hope we might be able to pick up something in the morning before we took off, but this was certainly a God-given opportunity. We managed to attract Mr. Walley to us while Dorothy was patting her pieces, told him of the birthday on the following day and asked if he would make this purchase for us on the side. In the accomplishment of this (and Dorothy's) deal Mr. Walley discovered, he told us later, the fine craftsman could neither read nor write.

As we three conspirators were shuffling out of the shed huddled around our scoop, we encountered Miss Lynam and Mr. Burrows coming ashore from their boat. They had waited to land until they had checked over the pictures they had, and what they wanted for the next day. They would like to inquire, Miss Lynam said, if they were not being too inquisitive, in what particular activity we three were engaged at the moment that required such conspicuously close companionship. They were charmed to hear about the birthday and the purchase and took up a stand at the door to the shed promising to engage Dorothy and Howard in conversation until we should have hidden our purchase in the car.

Less than two minutes of travel on the highway in the car suffused me in such fright and sweat I had to ask for help. Cars were roaring at us beyond the limit permitted on a speedway. Our driver was either a maniac or had lost control of his machine. I had to find out and if he were not conscious someone else must take the wheel.

"Please," I managed to say though my jaws were clenched, "can you go more slowly?" The driver looked back at me and at that I very nearly screamed. "Why, madam," he said, "we're only doing twenty-five." Dorothy and Arthur were in the car with me. Dorothy patted my knee.

"I should have warned you," she said, "I thought I'd die the first evening we drove from the boat. It's because we do three miles an hour all day and we don't see anything going faster. There's nothing you can do about it. You just suffer." Then I remembered it had been like this on the drive to Llangollen. I apologized to the driver and shut my eyes.

CHAPTER THIRTEEN

WE RETURNED to the Grand Hotel in Rugby where we had spent the preceding night. Our itinerary was a corroboration of the speed at which we traveled. We had gone from Brinklow to Braunston, each of these easily less than an hour's motoring from Rugby. We had left our bags at the hotel and it was pleasant not to have to unpack. Sophy, Dorothy, Howard and I came downstairs immediately and simultaneously for cocktails. We decided to wait for Arthur, but it was some time before he joined us. When he finally came into the bar Dorothy asked him where he had been. He hoped we would not consider it an indelicacy, he said, but since she had put such a direct question he must answer in kind, that he had been looking for a bathroom.

"I found it too," he boasted, "but I started in the wrong direction and got into a kind of mole run; different levels, odd turnings. The landlord found me. He got me out of there. I told him this is a 2T hotel in my book. We got quite friendly while he was leading me out of that labyrinth, but when I asked him what time he would like me to take my bath, he went all 'British ha-ha.' Said he enjoyed our American humor. I wasn't giving him any humor. The English are unpredictable."

When Howard asked why on earth the landlord should give advice about the time to bathe, Arthur looked from one to another of us, wide-eyed.

"Don't you all do that?" he asked. "Isn't it like a boat when you haven't a private bath, and the steward reserves a time for you? I've been asking every night as soon as we got into a hotel. Come to think of it," he added reflectively, "nobody has answered me."

Telling him this wasn't customary at a hotel, and a proprietor must have thought it an odd question, made Arthur defensive.

"How was I to know?" he demanded. "When I was a child we were too poor to go to a hotel, and by the time I could afford it I could afford a private bath. Except on boats."

Howard and Dorothy informed him with some vehemence that if he had ever gone on the road with a play in the old days, he would have known about hotel rooms without a bath. You didn't need an ocean liner to acquire that knowledge.

I broke in with the assertion I'd known plenty of bathless rooms on a lecture tour, but I did not know what a 2T hotel was.

"It's my own classification," Arthur said, a little smugly. "I make a note of it every night in my diary. 2T stands for two towels in your room. That's pretty good. It's the most we've had."

According to the original lineup of the crew Howard was the banker, I knew. I was not prepared to find him bartender as well, but as Arthur and I were talking, Howard went to the bar, spoke to the bartender, and at a gesture of welcome, joined him behind the counter, took the bottles of gin and vermouth his host provided, and began to prepare Martinis. The bartender, watching, stiffened to a hypnotic rigidity.

"I thought you were the wine steward," I said to Sophy. She explained the fine distinction. "I provide liquor for the boat, but at an inn Howard tends bar. He always asks permission first and he always has a spellbound audience."

Howard spoke. "Now then," he said briskly, "you see that's the way my wife and I like a Martini. If you'll just double it please." The bartender answered in the far-off tone of one coming from a trance into an unrecognizable place. "Double the gin too?" he asked.

"Good Lord yes," was Howard's answer. As Howard left, I saw the bartender pick up the bottle of gin in a hand that trembled visibly.

Joining us Howard shuddered as he sat down. "I fix one cocktail apiece for Dorothy and me," he said in a low tone. "Ask him to double it so that we can have two each and he wants to double just the vermouth."

"Everywhere we go," Dorothy observed sadly, "we shock a bartender." Turning to Arthur: "Day before yesterday you asked for a Bloody Mary and everyone in the whole room stopped talking."

"I know bloody isn't a word to use freely in England," Arthur protested, "but that was what I wanted. I thought of asking for a Sanguinary Mary but I thought he might not understand it. He didn't understand it anyway," Arthur added gloomily. "Howard had to show him."

"I think the ingredients shocked him more than the word," Howard asserted and shook his head. "No matter how hard we try; we dress properly, nothing loud, we never raise our voices, but we produce shocks."

We continued to impose our involuntary shock treatment. The next morning at breakfast I asked the waiter for a glass of water. In England a glass of water is provided automatically only in the most cosmopolitan restaurants. Elsewhere one must ask for it. We Americans for the most part do not realize how strange our habit is. A Frenchman told me one time the custom he found most difficult to reconcile with the American temperament of warmhearted hospitality was a glass of ice water offered as a *welcome* to a dining table.

I shocked the waiter by asking for a glass of water.

"Certainly, madam," he answered and left but returned almost immediately. "Hot?" he inquired. "No," I told him, "cold, very cold."

He brought me a pitcher of it so deliciously cold it did not need ice and certainly it had none. Presently a man and a woman sat down at a table near ours. The man was the embodiment of caricatures of a British Army officer, stocky, ruddy face, bristling mustache, rigid carriage. I expected to hear him speak in a tone that would have carried across a parade ground. But of course I had forgotten that in public places, particularly hotel dining rooms, English people speak so quietly their words are not audible however close together the tables are placed. I see their lips move, but I have never caught a sound. Perhaps they communicate by lip reading. By whatever fashion they establish communication with one another the man gave an order to our mutual waiter. The waiter came to my table, asked if he might take the pitcher of water he had placed there. He filled the Brigadier General or whatever's glass. With a silent acknowledgment, Old Ironsides drank from it. The silence of that room was splintered by a bellow of words that would certainly have reached the farthest corner of a parade ground. "Good God, the water's *cold*." The waiter looked at me reproachfully and moved his lips rapidly to the outraged guest.

A few minutes later Dorothy joined me, and Sophy followed, tiptoeing around Arthur and Howard, whom I had previously skirted. There was a plate of toast on our table. It had been there when I arrived. If the slices beneath were like the one on top they were all burned. Dorothy touched delicately the one in view. "Stone cold," she said. The waiter came to take her order, and Sophy's. When Sophy had finished Dorothy asked, "And could we have some fresh toast, do you think?" "Certainly, madam," the waiter answered and removed the plate. He came back almost immediately, leaned over Dorothy and inquired, "Hot?" Dorothy could not conceal her astonishment. "Why yes," she told him. "Thank you, madam," the waiter answered and went away again, shaking his head.

Presently the men came over with hearty greetings and expressions of pleasure at their first sight of us. Asked about their health and general well-being, Arthur reported though he had slept well he had been nervously startled during his breakfast and newspaper by, of all things, a loud noise in an English dining room, a profane shout of anger from one of its patrons. I told them in a whisper about the water and Dorothy shared the episode of the toast.

181

Both the men requested us in the future not to be such iconoclasts.

Our departure from the hotel was appreciably delayed because Howard had to pay a bill of two days. This was the first time I had seen our banker actually filling his office. The inauguration of a President, the opening of Parliament is done with not much greater circumstance, I think, than accompanied our financial director in his dispensations of the community fund of the crew.

We were asked to assemble in the Lindsays' room. Howard would obtain the bill at the desk and then join us. The moment he came in we knew he was a troubled man. Dorothy asked anxiously if the bill was exorbitant. He assured her it was not, adding as a matter of fact he hadn't looked at it yet. "But," he explained mournfully, "on the way up I realized I have made a grave blunder. I need your help and I owe you a deep apology. I feel sure you will want someone else to take over my post and I do not blame you."

"Horse racing?" Arthur inquired with a gleam in his eye. Howard shook his head. "It is a confusion of pockets," he explained. "Due to the painted utensils last night." This was evidently as ambiguous to the others as it was to me. No one spoke until Arthur started on another tack. "Did you use up all the money? I didn't think they were so expen—" He broke off with a yelp because Sophy had kicked him sharply in the shin. She did not wish him to reveal we knew the cost because we had purchased one of these for Dorothy's birthday. Howard had paid no attention and Dorothy was watching him anxiously. He continued, "I've kept the general fund and my own money in separate wallets and in separate pockets, but last night I must have been carried away by Dorothy's excitement. This is the only way I can account for such carelessness. I paid for those purchases from the wallet in the wrong pocket. I propose now to empty the contents of each wallet on each of our beds. You all know how much money you put in. I have kept carefully the bill from the preceding lodgings and I have written down our shopping expenditures. I haven't included the tips but they have caused me always such anxiety that I think I can remember them. I also know how much of my own money I should have."

In spite of our protests to skip the whole thing, Howard spread over the surface of each bed the contents of the two wallets, counted the money and noted the amount on a piece of paper. This took a considerable time because to evaluate the silver money he had to hold each piece close to his eyes and push his glasses down on his nose in order to read the identification of English currency.

He was not making appreciable progress in his computation when Dorothy gave a happy cry. "Why, Howard," she said, "I have the bill for the painted pieces. Don't you remember? Mr. Walley wrote it all down because the craftsman couldn't read or write." Howard accepted gratefully the piece of paper she produced from her bag. He took from the bed that displayed his personal fund the amount stipulated, reading each coin as he extracted it. He carried this sum to the other bed, and made a deposit there. When the money from each bed had been deposited in its proper wallet, the wallet deposited in the proper pocket, we were ready for the bill. Our banker went over the items quickly and efficiently. "It seems all right to me," he pro- nounced, and cowering a little inquired, "Do you want me to add it up?"

We assured him in vehement chorus we wanted no such operation, knowing neither he nor any one of us had the faintest idea of what to put down and what to carry over in terms of pence, shillings, pounds. Howard was per- ceptibly relieved. "All right then," he said. "It's all taken care of except the tip; that always makes me anxious." I would have said there were a number of things under the general heading of banking that caused him anxiety, but I did not point this out, feeling Howard after all probably knew better than I his personal scale of anxieties. Once more the wallet came out of the pocket, contents were spread across the bed; Howard surveyed the assortment somberly. Sophy ventured a suggestion; I thought this forward of her, but Howard seized it gratefully and the pieces of money she indicated. These isolated, he put the remainder in the wallet, the wallet in the pocket. We went downstairs; he paid the bill, tipped appropriately judging from the warm but not exaggerated gratitude expressed and we were on our way once more.

At the dock we found Miss Lynam and Mr. Burrows on the lookout for us. They drew me aside immediately.

"We managed to get some champagne for Miss Stickney's birthday," Miss Lynam said. "Do you think you could smuggle it on board and get it into her cooling contrap- tion?" They took it from their boat and I carried it on board the *Maid Marysue*.

I was surprised not to see Mr. Walley and Mr. Fitter at the engine or on the dock on the lookout to help us

184

aboard with our bags, but when I entered the main cabin I saw them with their backs to me bending over the dining table already let down from the wall. They both jumped when I spoke to them, whirling around guiltily. Seeing who it was they relaxed and moved to either side, exposing in the center of the table a vase containing half a dozen carnations. I learned they had hitched a ride into town early that morning, waited until the florist had opened and made this purchase; the more touching because the fields were spilling over with flowers. They could have had an armload for the asking from any householder along the road, but they wanted to show, I'm sure, not that they had brought something for her birthday, but made a purchase. I was assuring them the sparse little bunch was beautiful and that Miss Stickney would be overcome, and indeed I knew she would be touched.

Sophy and Arthur sidled through the door, the painted scoop between them. They were put out with me, and they conveyed this articulately, because I had forgotten to take our present from the car. By the time Sophy remembered, and fetched it, I had disappeared, leaving the two of them to convey it without Dorothy's notice. They had accomplished this because Arthur had been inspired to engage Sophy in an extraordinary kind of dance that had necessitated their wrapping their arms around each other's necks, the vessel between them, and proceeding past Dorothy sideways in an elaborate grapevine step. Dorothy had been charmed, but Sophy was full of complaints. She had been made to look a fool in the eyes of other spectators, cruisers who had come ashore and been as interested as Dorothy. They were mollified when I called their attention to the flowers and put into benign humor when I told them of the champagne waiting to go in Dorothy's cooler.

We made a fine display on the table with little oddments we had picked up as fun gifts all heaped around the centerpiece of carnations. Howard, cued by Sophy, had kept Dorothy as long as possible on the dock by persuading her to return to the sheds on the chance there might be other painted tins available, hoping fervently, as he admitted later, against such misfortune. He was cast down at the prospect of the shipment already accumulated.

No child could have shown surprise and pleasure so spontaneously and generously as Dorothy gave us from the doorway of the cabin. She had not known any of us was aware this was her birthday. We had been careful not to include mention of it in our "good mornings," though Arthur had come perilously close to it. When the men had come to our table to bestow on us their recognition, Arthur had uttered the syllable "Ha—" but Sophy had pressed her foot firmly on his instep and he had stopped talking altogether. Later, limping a little as we went upstairs for the bankers' convention, he had inquired of Sophy why she had chosen to injure him deliberately.

"Because," she said, "you were about to say happy birthday." Arthur had stopped so abruptly I behind him very nearly did an involuntary leapfrog. Dorothy and Howard had preceded us and were out of hearing. Arthur had turned indignantly to Sophy.

"Happy birthday?" he had echoed a little shrilly. "I never thought of such a thing. I'd forgotten until this instant it was anybody's birthday."

"What were you going to say, then?" Sophy demanded.

186

"Have you any cigarettes?" Arthur answered. "But thank you very much I don't care for one now." Sophy had apologized earnestly, Arthur had been magnanimous.

Dorothy's pleasure in our water scoop was enriched she admitted because its appearance had solved a disappearance that had perplexed her the night before and that she'd found herself frequently running over in her mind. She was sure she had seen a water scoop and had had every intention of adding it to her purchases, but when she had turned from her contemplation of the other pieces, the object she was positive she had caught sight of was no longer there. She had not examined it closely, therefore she could not positively assert where it had been; on the other hand, she was equally positive she had seen a piece on the spot that was then empty.

Having got the scoop on board and surprised Dorothy with it, and with the other evidences of her birthday, our next problem was to remove her from them in order to secrete the champagne in the cooler. I accomplished this separation by urging her to hurry into her change of costume and come on the roof; I had a story I was longing to tell. The episode of her toast at breakfast had reminded me of it.

I have never met anyone of the theater who does not love to hear and tell a story. This does not surprise me; what bewilders me is the number of people who are indifferent to anecdotes. Certainly I am not one of these. I love to hear stories. I do not limit this to an enjoyment of a "joke." Actually, my greater enjoyment is in the recital of an episode, a narrative. I even like to hear people tell me about their trips. I would have listened by the hour to Odysseus' story of his travels, but the only dependable group for reciprocal enjoyment comes from the theater. Therefore Howard and Arthur came with Dorothy and, bless them, even *asked* me to tell the story I'd had in mind. It was an incident that had happened years ago when I had been in England with my family and I'm glad I remembered it because it provided a useful and comforting slogan we employed for the rest of the cruise. To this day, mentioning it brings back memories of English country inns.

On that far-off trip at dusk one evening, I had come into my father's room at the hotel in London where we were staying. He had been standing at the window looking out and I had gone across the room and slipped my arm through his. Seeing with him the lights coming on over the city I had said, "Isn't it beautiful? What a city!" And my father had answered, "Yes it is, but actually what I was thinking about was that all over the country at this very moment English people are making their toast for tomorrow's breakfast."

Sophy had stayed in the cabin to store the champagne. When she joined us on the roof Dorothy jumped up apologetically and in dismay that she had forgotten to store the perishables in her container and put away supplies. In spite of Sophy's assurance it had all been done, Dorothy was insistent on making sure the container was properly sealed until Howard asked me to repeat to Sophy my incident of the toast. Another trait of theater people I happen to know and that I find particularly endearing is they do not mind hearing a story again, and since this is precisely my own feeling, I consider the trait both compatible and endearing. Dorothy immediately settled down to hear the anecdote once more. It would not have occurred to her, and Howard knew this, to leave just because she had already heard it only some three minutes before.

We kept her out of reach of the container for the entire morning by stories alternated with reading aloud from *Tom Brown's School Days.* Howard had found a copy of the classic in a Rugby bookshop and we were all reading it with a happy surprise at its excellence. Howard pointed out it was somewhat naïve of us to be surprised. A book reprinted and read over one hundred years might be assumed to have some excellence. Not one of us had been able to name the author. And even when we read Thomas Hughes on the jacket no one was able to say, "Oh, of course."

We had become wary of laying bets on knowledge because Howard invariably won. He had made a cleaning in Coventry, been right both about the reason Lady Godiva rode through its streets just as she was and that the original Peeping Tom had been the citizen who had presumed to look and gone blind as a result. He had also known the origin of "being sent to Coventry." This had been the last time we had fattened his personal wallet. Since then each of us had been reticent about asserting his knowledge. Howard was inclined to be reproachful at our becoming taciturn, pleading this same wallet was being so consistently thinned by Arthur's prowess at gin it would be only fair if we would help him to regain both an economic balance and one of self-confidence.

At Napton Locks, Arthur and Howard went ashore with Mr. Fitter to help at the gates. Dorothy was amenable to Sophy's suggestion we join them and walk a bit. Like jailers, though she did not know this, we escorted her to the towpath. We conceded to the men at work little cries of admiration at their dexterity. We would have bestowed them more lavishly had the men not been the first to request them. They had become skillful and quick, and

this proved, I said, anyone after a little practice can take a boat through the canals without professional assistance. I pointed out to my companions, but in a low tone, I would find it impossible to designate two men I would have considered more backward about any form of navigation than the two we now saw nimbly winding and dropping paddles and pushing gates. Dorothy speculated aloud on the possibility of diverting this newly discovered adroitness to usefulness around the house, but decided this went beyond probability. Actually, she told Sophy, she was going to have to put Howard through a rigorous drill when they got home to get back to such practical responsibilities as he had formerly assumed, because he was now so spoiled by Sophy's solicitous attendance what with the newspaper every morning, crawling under the table every noon, and general waiting on the males. Sophy accepted the rebuke but made no promise to change her ways.

There are bridges beyond the Napton Locks and when we had passed the second of these the conspirators decided we had found a charming spot for lunch. Dorothy was pleased at the suggestion we vary our program by lunching on shore that day. But when she saw that the centerpiece of our tablecloth on the grass was the vase of flowers with a bottle of champagne on either side of it, she spread around us again the heartwarming rapture of a child surprised.

That was a day to remember; warm sun making patterns through the leaves of the big tree under which we sat, a lark in the sky, bullfinches darting like bright arrows around a bush not far off, the canal beside us, the champagne almost cold. Arthur opened it steadily in spite of our shrill suggestions and advice. We all shared it, though Mr. Burrows was taking so many pictures I doubt he gave himself time for more than a sip.

Even such a gala did not divert the men from their game of gin once we were on board again, nor did it divert

Arthur from winning as usual. When they joined us on the roof an appraisal of Howard's melancholy and Arthur's embarrassment was not difficult. Dorothy scarcely paused in her lubrication and costume application. "Arthur," she said severely, "you've won again. And on my birthday!"

CHAPTER FOURTEEN

At about five o'clock we were at Fenny Compton. When we pulled in there we said to one another this day's run on the Oxford Canal had been one of the most beautiful on the trip, winding, since it was a Brindley design, through a gentle landscape Constable might have painted. We had seen a windmill on a distant hill, lost it, seen it again in half an hour when our canal had curved that way again. Throughout a great part of the day the mill and a distant farmhouse had been disappearing and recurring landmarks.

We set our own landmark at Fenny Compton. Madame Pandit with the two of her three daughters who were with her in London was to join us the next morning for a day's cruise. We were to telephone her that night the meeting place. We selected a pub called the George and Dragon. It stood on the highway at the end of a steep path that led up from the canal.

We had a few anxious moments on our arrival at the Craven Arms in Southam where we were to spend the night. We had come by car from Fenny Compton where there is no inn. We did not recognize in our landlord a jokester.

There had been no difficulty at any inn about our reservations. Each evening we had found ready for us either one double room and three singles, or two double rooms, Sophy and I sharing, and a single. Our only exaction had been separate beds in each room. But the landlord at Southam said, as Howard was signing the register:

"Now who is having my big room with the double bed accommodations?"

Howard's nervous start made a blot on the page of the ledger.

"Double bed?" he repeated anxiously. "No, no. There must be some mistake. Mrs. Lindsay and I have said all along we have to have two beds. Neither of us sleeps well under the best circumstances. This would be impossible."

Dorothy joined him at the desk. Arthur, Sophy and I listened from the foot of the stairs, sitting on our suitcases. Several guests in the lounge adjoining were interested too, we could see.

Dorothy smiled winningly at our host. "We really do have to have two beds," she coaxed.

"That room," the landlord boomed at his audience, "is big enough to ride a bicycle in."

Howard's face reddened. He spoke quietly but with deadly enunciation.

"I do not wish to ride a bicycle," he said, "and neither does Mrs. Lindsay."

"Well you could if you'd a mind to," the landlord answered.

I think Howard was on the verge of giving a list of

things he might have a mind to do that under no possibility would include bicycling. The landlord forestalled him. With a sudden and unexpected roar of laughter, and a slap on his thigh, he said, "I was only giving you an idea of the size of the room I've got for you. Big enough for a bicycle ride, and so it's big enough to hold TWO double beds, and that's what it's got."

He was still laughing at his own wit when he showed them into the room. It was large, it did hold two double beds, but it would not have afforded much in the way of a bicycle route.

We were surprised too by our landlord's wife. She came into the bar while Howard was educating the bartender in Lindsay Martinis. She wore a bright-flowered chintz skirt, an off-the-shoulder blouse with full sleeves, many necklaces and large hoops in her ears. We thought she was a gypsy, but she was miffed when Arthur asked if she read palms or tea leaves. Howard covered our embarrassment at learning her identity by asking her to try one of his cocktails. She did and progressed from being appeased to a warm appreciation of our company in a remarkably short time.

After dinner Sophy telephoned Madame Pandit in London, told her how beautiful the days had been, this one the peak of them all. Tomorrow would be just like it. Madame Pandit was delighted with the place for our meeting. "The girls and I will be outside the pub at nine o'clock tomorrow morning. It's a pity some members of the Diplomatic Corps won't see us."

The call completed, we went on our customary evening's exploring tour, but unlike our custom, traveled only a short distance. A few yards down the road from our hotel we saw on a swinging signboard THE OLD MINT INN and promptly made this the evening's exploration.

The Old Mint Inn is a stunning old pub of the sixteenth century with oak paneling that rivals Plas Newydd's in Llangollen. What space is not occupied by this, and even covering some of it, is a collection of copper and brasses and harnesses. The floor space was very nearly as solidly packed with people. We threaded our way among the tables and discovered a beautifully carved staircase leading to the upper floor. We encountered the proprietor at the foot of this, but he declared himself too busy to show us the way, and waved us on to discover for ourselves. There were more pieces on the walls and on tables about the low-ceilinged rooms upstairs. We investigated them happily although Dorothy was a little piqued to learn nothing could be purchased. "Even though," she pointed out, "it's my birthday." We stopped downstairs for a glass of beer and then went outside for further exploring. We found a small, old church across the road from our inn and walked around it, though at ten o'clock at night obviously it was locked and we could not see the interior. In England it is not more than dusk at that hour, with a soft pale light. We were reluctant to go to bed.

The next morning when Arthur acknowledged the existence of women in his party, he told us he might as well have stayed in the church yard enjoying the scene and the night. He had enjoyed no part of it from his bed though he had been aware of each passing hour. He had been even more acutely aware of each passing truck on the highway directly below his window. At dawn he had made a correction in his diary. He had demoted the Craven Arms from 2 to 1½T.

We were at the George and Dragon pub at the side of what Sophy had identified to Madame Pandit as a "hump-backed bridge" by nine o'clock the next morning. Less than a quarter of an hour later the Indian Embassy car drove up reminding us of a style we had left far behind and almost forgotten. Madame Pandit descended from it followed by her oldest daughter Lehka and her youngest Rita. They were delighted with our boat, though Arthur at the top of the path had warned them at first sight of it he had considered it an approximate size to a lifeboat on the *Queen Mary*. Madame Pandit, in spite of her sari, leapt aboard far more nimbly than I was ever able to accomplish even in slacks. Lehka was dressed like her mother, but Rita wore slacks, purchased she said the day before especially for this occasion. She was looking forward to climbing about the boat, and on and off it to walk along the towpath as we had described.

We were no sooner settled on our cushions on the roof when the sky began to cloud over and within a few moments drops of rain fell. The visitors brushed these aside; certainly they would not go below, each of them declared, and the rest of us with insincere positiveness assured one another this was only a little shower.

It was a shower that lasted the entire day. The only aspect about it that changed was its progress from a faint spatter to a steady downpour. For a time with raincoats, blankets and scarves we faced it from the roof, but before lunch we surrendered and retreated to the main cabin. We had planned to make another picnic on the bank because of

198

the success of the one the day before, but there would have been nothing of success or pleasure in wet food on wet ground. Happily the food was good and our guests in such high spirits the meal was a gala. India's High Commissioner away from her office and its duties was in a gay holiday mood, and no one among my friends is a gayer companion than she. Her daughters have her capacity for enjoyment and so we did not allow the rain to matter although of course it did. Most of the things Sophy and I had held out as inducements were washed out. This was the only day of the two weeks on the *Maid Marysue* the sun did not shine.

After lunch, while Dorothy washed up, Arthur and Howard excused themselves. We saw them next through the open door to a forward cabin, Arthur on a stool, Howard on the lower bunk and doubled far over because the upper bunk would not permit him to sit straight. They held a suitcase between them on their knees. They were playing gin. Madame Pandit had a nap on the couch in the main cabin. Rita, Lehka, Sophy and I played Scrabble. Later in the afternoon in spite of the downpour we walked along the towpath to watch the operation of putting the *Maid Marysue* through a lock.

We came into Banbury about teatime. The Embassy car was waiting and our dampened excursionists went back to London.

We said good-by, too, to Miss Lynam and Mr. Burrows, and with genuine regret. We had been somewhat churlish about their coming because we had anticipated an intrusion of strangers would be bothersome. They had not intruded. Mr. Burrows had loped along the towpath, Miss

Lynam for most of the time had remained on their own boat taking notes. When they had joined us it had been at our invitation and they had brought gaiety and easy companionship, plus two bottles of champagne on the special occasion. As we said good-by we promised a reunion in London and they in turn guaranteed each of us would have copies of such photographs as we wanted for souvenirs of the voyage.

CHAPTER FIFTEEN

W E SPENT the night in the Crown Hotel at
Banbury in Oxfordshire. That hostelry merited, Arthur
said, 2½ T in his listing. In spite of the remoteness of the
bathrooms from our sleeping apartments and the labyrin-
thian passages that connected them, we had two towels
each, and he had slept well. I had opportunity for
long conversation with the landlord, who was not a jokester, because the others of the crew abandoned me and
went off to Stratford by car to see a performance of *As
You Like It.* They had decided for me a program of early
to bed because of the wet day in order to avoid recurrence
of the flu.

Almost immediately after their departure, the sky cleared
and the sun came out. I explored the town a little and did
some shopping. By coincidence, of our crew of five, two
had very nearly adjacent birthdays. Sophy's would be on
the following day, the 23rd. I discovered Market Day was
just closing. All round the square merchants were emptying their booths, but the wares still displayed made a
bright showing. Narrow, winding streets circled three-

quarters of the square like spokes from the hub of a wheel. The other section fanned out into a broad thoroughfare. I bought some gay and foolish gifts.

The landlord talked with me as I was having dinner. He had come to report the champagne the gentlemen had ordered for the following day was now in cold storage. I was happy to learn the precedent of champagne celebration was to be maintained. This matter concluded, we moved on to talk about food. He told me the price of vegetables was scandalously high because of the continued drought and that frozen foods were not available. He assured me it would be a difficult year for all innkeepers although this should be their most profitable season. When I suggested the very drought would perhaps bring more guests than usual since continuous sunny weather was an irresistible inducement to taking a trip, he agreed. Nevertheless he insisted the over-all price for lodging could not be boosted sufficiently to outweigh the deficit food costs would bring.

When he left me to take care of other customers, I realized our talk about food had let me know why during this cruise and the preceding one Sophy and I had taken, I had been haunted by will-o'-the-wisp thoughts of my childhood. They had darted in and out my mind. More than once I had been puzzled about why I had been sharply reminded of the little town where I was born or an inconsequential incident that had happened there. Now I recognized the association. For many years like almost all other Americans I had not marked a change of season by particular food or fruit. String beans in New York are as easy to purchase in January as in July, but in my childhood food was as indicative of the time of year as the temperature. If Mrs. Ball telephoned my mother to say "I'm at the Sterling. Mr. Anderson has peas. I've told him to put half a peck aside for you," Mother would hurry downtown to claim them and we would know "Sumer was icumen in." Now all the years later and in England I was harking back to Muncie, Indiana. In rural England, beans, peas, asparagus, strawberries are not flown from far-off places to local markets. The housewife buys what the season offers.

Because of their evening in the outside world that had kept them up late, the crew was not aboard the *Maid Marysue* the next morning until ten o'clock. The sky was cloudless, the sun warm; it was like every other day except the one we had particularly wanted to be bright. This time there was no package so large as the dipper to smuggle on board. However, Sophy was isolated, to allow the champagne to be put in the cooler, by the simple expedient of my becoming disagreeable as we were putting supplies in the cupboard. I said I was sick and tired of being shunted off from the galley; by the precedent of previous trips it was my own milieu. I had counted accurately on Sophy's characteristic of departing hastily from a spot where sparks are flying. She left the cabin on the double and took to the roof. I promised Dorothy correctly we could wrap up the little presents, make all preparations uninterrupted; Sophy would not return. The only interruptions were from each other. It was impossible not to look out the window and call the other's attention to the passing scene. This might include a family of moorhens, the parents hysterically gathering in the little ones and then changing their minds and directions with a difference of opinion between them as to the best hiding place, or it was a flash of blue that a king-fisher in his swift flight seemed to have left behind.

Sometimes we moved out to stand beside Mr. Walley and Mr. Fitter in order to see the full oval of a bridge as we neared it, the reflection in the still water inverting and completing the arch above. Mr. Walley had taught us to look for a deep groove on the towpath side of bridges. It was the mark, he said, of the rope, from the days when barges were horse-drawn. So many barges running in the old days of heavy traffic on these waters, so many horses walking the path as it skirted around and under a bridge, had worn deep into the stone the mark of their passing. In those days, he had told us too, when the canals were crowded and competition high, horses were changed almost in midstream; at least alongside, as they walked along, without halting the barge.

Once we came out at a run in answer to a hail from both helmsmen. We saw the *Maid Marysue,* like the Queen reviewing a troop, was about to pass a long row of fishermen that stretched ahead of us as far as we could see. Each member of this company, and it did not include a woman, was seated at a precise and uniform distance from his neighbor. He sat on a folding chair with an open black umbrella lashed to the back. The line from every fishing rod extended almost exactly the same distance into the canal. As we approached each one in turn it did not move until we were very nearly over it. Then it would be reluctantly withdrawn by its disgruntled owner, who scowled at our invasion. A few times, Dorothy and I essayed a timid "good morning," and more infrequently we were granted an acknowledgment. Mr. Walley explained this was a weekly fishing contest held every Sunday during the season, and a solemn occasion—that was a superfluous detail we did not need to be told. Rules established the distance between anglers and there were many other regulations. He explained these things in a whisper, and when Dorothy and I returned to the cabin, we tiptoed.

We had finished our work as we reached the locks at Aynho at a little before one o'clock, and we joined the others on the towpath. We found them talking to a couple from a "pleasure craft," as the British call them, like ours. These cruisers said the village was well worth stopping off to see, and was only a short distance from the canal.

We decided instantly and unanimously to visit Aynho village. The lock to our astonishment was operated by a keeper, so no help was needed from our crew. We went up the bank from the towpath, crossed a bridge and reaching a highway turned left as we had been directed. We came almost immediately in sight of a railway station on a high embankment to our right and said cheerfully to one another the village must of course be at this spot.

The town of Aynho is a full mile, perhaps a little more, from its station, and I do not know the reason for this gap of open country. (Note: never accept literally a British estimate of "only a step," or "just up the road.") We were hot, dusty and Howard's feet hurt. These observations were made frequently. Nevertheless we forgot our discomfort at the sight of a pair of tall gates, a driveway on the other side and on the gates a notice that Aynhoe Park was open from April until September daily including Sundays from 11 to 6.

We paid our admission fee of two and six each to a charming gentleman. We were the only visitors so he summoned a maid, turned over admissions to her and led us through the house. The name Aynho, he told us, is from a Saxon word Aienho that means "spring or grove on a hill" and the foundations of the seventeenth-century mansion, Aynhoe Park, are of the original Norman castle. The village itself has retained its original circular shape and sections of the high wall can still be seen.

Since the latter part of the sixteenth century the house, Aynhoe Park, has belonged to the Cartwright family in unbroken succession. We had seen, as we crossed a magnificent courtyard, the outline of the house was of a center section three stories high with a long low wing on either side, the wings obviously added at a later date but with a

206

uniformity of style to give the whole an Elizabethan character. The visitors' entrance leads immediately into a small lobby, and this opens into the Chinese rooms. Our guide told us the original rooms had been remodeled to accommodate a collection of Chinese and Persian ceramics and glass the present owner had acquired and assembled. We spent a considerable time here, delighting in the exquisite pieces.

From these rooms by way of a narrow passage and an elevation of three steps we came into a picture gallery officially called the Murillo room because of a predominance of pictures by that artist. The greater part of the furniture is seventeenth-century Italian and Spanish. This room in turn leads to the French drawing room by a descent of three steps. From the top of these we looked down on a vista of succeeding rooms. In the dining room the table was set with magnificent china. We were told one of the treasures is the "Waterloo Service" of Meissen. The history of this is it was left on the battlefield of Waterloo by Napoleon and found there by General William Cartwright. The glass on the table, eighteenth-century Venetian, and the gold urn that was its centerpiece had been presented to a General Cartwright by George III.

The library very nearly caused a mutiny from two members of our crew. Had Arthur and Howard believed they might remain, either with permission or secreted, I think they would have abandoned the *Maid Marysue* and us. With low moans of pleasure they moved from shelf to shelf of this glorious room and with the guide's permission fingered lovingly one volume after another. I was dimly aware I caught our mentor looking from one to another of us with what seemed to me a puzzled scrutiny. When one of us called another's attention to a particular picture, identifying its painter, or a book, talking of it with affectionate familiarity, he affirmed what we said and joined in our discussion cordially but with an abstractedness. My nebulous impressions were not sharpened into understanding until we came out into the front hall after we had made the complete circuit of the rooms. Here in a niche with special lighting from above was the most dramatic flower arrangement I think I have ever seen. The urn from which rose towering stalks of brilliant blue delphinium, with lilies below, then a massing of color, was itself at least four feet high. The effect was dramatic but not flamboyant. Recessed, it was like a vivid tapestry on a wall.

With a gasp, Dorothy pointed. "I have never in my life seen anything like that," she said. "I'll never forget it." In the hand with which she pointed hung as dismal a little flower arrangement as I know I have ever seen. She had gathered a few wildflowers and weeds as we had trudged up the road. They were all wilted. Every member of the sparse little bunch hung limply from her fist over the back of her hand. With dreadful shock I knew why we had puzzled our guide. We were dressed in our boating outfits. Each of these was the quintessence of what I had vehemently deplored in Sophy's New York apartment in February.

"I beg of you," I had said, "let's never step ashore until we are properly dressed for it."

We were not only ashore, we were in one of the handsomest of England's historic houses and this is how we were dressed: Dorothy, along with her bunch of flowers, was wearing a pale blue full cotton skirt that had not been put on fresh that morning. Her blouse was topped by a bright red sweater buttoned all the way up. She had protected her lower extremities with white wool knee socks and a pair of dark blue canvas espadrilles. I knew they were dark blue because I had seen them before but at first view, such as our guide's, they must have seemed something between beige and gray because they were encased in dust from the road. Arthur was in blue slacks of a paler shade than Dorothy's skirt. His rubber-soled shoes matched. Over the top of his dark blue sweater a rumpled collar of a pale blue sport shirt could be seen. In his hand he carried a dark blue cotton cap with an exaggerated visor. Howard's shoes were pale blue canvas, his trousers were gray, his sweater, buttoned all the way, was dark blue. His shirt, with open collar, was blue-and-white check; his cap was white. My slacks were dark blue and not so long as they should have been; therefore they exposed a considerable section of white wool socks. My canvas shoes were light blue too and over my sport shirt I was wearing a confection I had purchased in New York and at the time had thought natty. It was an over jacket that zipped up the front from bottom to top much in the manner of the upper part of children's two-piece snow suits. The material was nylon and the color pale blue-and-white check. It was guaranteed to be rainproof and also, in spite of its lightness, to have considerable warmth. It had fulfilled both these guarantees, but it also fulfilled a promise it could be worn over other jackets; therefore it had somewhat the dimensions of an open parachute.

Sophy's rig, however, was the real gem of the ocean. The rest of us thought she had coaxed it from a switchman in a railway yard, the only environment in which any of us had seen its duplicate. When Sophy had learned our assumption she was indignant. She had bought it she declared at one of the smartest shops in New York and furthermore had had several fittings, I cannot think where. It was of dark blue heavy denim, the weight of workmen's overalls. It included slacks and coat to match. The sum of its parts was over-all bagginess, although a sense of fairness nags me to admit each of us drooped in the seat. I wonder we had been admitted by way of the front door, but I do not wonder our guide was startled and bemused by an indication of familiarity with the things we saw. I have an uncomfortable conviction, too, the reason he turned over his post at the turnstile to someone else and accompanied us personally was not at a prospect of intellectual congeniality but of some of the treasures being swiped.

The realization of the way we looked had come to each of us on the instant Dorothy extended her posies. We had looked at one another with anything but a wild surmise. We knew precisely where and how we stood. The only thing worse than our appearance would have been an apology or an explanation, but we expressed our gratitude singly and in chorus with a fervor that sounded, I thought, a little pathetic. We scuttled across the elegant courtyard down the driveway and out the gate and immediately we were beyond it Dorothy threw away her wildflowers.

Nevertheless we decided it was no more inappropriate to visit the village than the "stately home," and perhaps since it was two o'clock most of the inhabitants would be either eating or napping.

It would have been a pity to turn back. The village is

a delight. There are scarcely more than one hundred cottages in all, most of them of pre-Tudor. Some of them still have an outside staircase. Another particular charm is the survival of a feudal custom. Apricot trees are grown on the walls of the houses dating from the time when the fruit was part of the rent payment to the lord of the manor. We saw dovecotes and tithe barns.

Sophy suggested beer at the end of our tour, even offering to treat. In fact she had begun suggesting it on our walk up the dusty hill even before we had reached Aynhoe Park. We had been noncommital then about our acceptance, thinking she would forget about it if we did not pursue the subject. That is, the others thought this would be so. Knowing Sophy over a far longer period than they have known her I knew she does not forget an idea once she has proposed it. I knew with equal sureness the only way to circumvent her was to evince a positive dislike of her suggestion. She is sensitively amenable to the preferences of others. The reason we wished to forestall her was the champagne waiting in the cooler.

Sophy was obviously disgruntled but even more perplexed by our adamant stand. It was not so much our turning against her as that we had turned away from our own natures. As we trudged the dusty way home Sophy reviewed this contradiction aloud from several aspects, none of them making any sense she said, particularly since Howard continued to complain his feet hurt. A long walk, a hot day, a dusty road, a dry throat, an offer of beer providing equally an opportunity for Howard to sit down and not have to pay so much as a shilling out of either pocket, and still he and the rest of us refused.

The sight of the bottles of champagne as a centerpiece on the table in our cabin was as instantly soothing to Sophy as a lollipop to a querulous child. Mr. Walley and Mr. Fitter in our absence had not only arranged the table but prepared lunch and added their own gift of flowers. Sophy was as pleased as Dorothy had been and equally surprised. We pointed out that surprise was something of an affectation, we thought, since she had remarked more than once, and pointedly, what a curious coincidence it was her birthday should occur only two days after Dorothy's.

Thanks to her own prompting we were even better prepared for this occasion than for the first. We not only had gifts, we had rhymes. Dorothy had purchased an autograph album and had each of us write in it a sentiment to Sophy. The first, a sort of chorus, signed by all of us, ran:

> *Hail to your birthday, Sophy Yarnall,* *
> *Our love for you is strictly carnal.*

A solo from Howard followed.

> *In skirts, in shorts, in all her make-ups,*
> *There is no girl like Sophy Jacobs.*

Arthur's even carried a title, "On This Your Natal Day."

> *You the cook, I the shirker,*
> *I the drone, you the worker,*
> *I the eater, you the maker,*
> *You the giver, I the taker,*
> *I the oaf, you my better,*
> *Aye, dear Sophy, I your debtor.*

* Sophy's maiden name.

Mine was poor. I am unable to compose so few as two lines in verse form, but Dorothy's was a gem that glittered brightest of all.

> *Sophy's rear beneath the table*
> *Makes us think of Betty Grable.*

Arthur had illustrated this vividly.

Arthur was the one, too, who told us the legend that was symbolized in a tiny silver cart driven by two oxen that was a joint gift with Howard. They had purchased it, Arthur said, in a little antique shop in Banbury and had been told it represented an old, old story of a squire, young, hot-blooded, and in love with a beautiful maiden whose cruel father had forbidden them to marry. Secretly they had made plans to elope but on the night appointed such a heavy snow fell as had never before been seen in that part of England. The distraught lover, knowing no horse and fine carriage in his stable could carry them in such weather, hit upon the plan of using instead a humble farm cart and a pair of sturdy oxen. The patient beasts struggled through the night and finally broke through the drifts to reach the trysting place just before dawn. The maiden was waiting half frozen. Her squire, disguised in rude clothing, placed her, well wrapped in warm fur robes, on the bottom of the cart, covered her with straw, and drove slowly away. No one suspected his identity, no one tried to stop them. Their unfrustrated and successful union marked the founding of a great house and line whose descendants incorporated in their coat of arms a cart and a pair of oxen like the one presented to Sophy.

On our return from the cruise I told many people about

Here, dear Sophie

Arthur Kober

the legend of Banbury, urging them when they went there to try to secure the little emblem of the place. When one of these friends wanted the name of the family I realized Arthur had never mentioned it so the next time I saw him I asked this information. He looked at me blankly a moment and then had the grace to be embarrassed. "Why," he admitted finally, "didn't you know? I made up the whole story. Howard and I thought there ought to be some reason for giving a little ornament that had no purpose."

From the number to whom I told it in a recital of our travels, I daresay the legend of Banbury is fairly widespread today.

Sophy made a birthday speech of course. People who know her family maintain it only requires two of its members to meet at lunch for each of them to toast and make a speech to the other. On her birthday Sophy spoke more than once, using as provocation an assumption of a different identity each time. First the recipient of birthday honors, then the cruise director, the map reader, and finally the cook. She was roundly applauded as each character.

When she had run out of characters, though certainly not of speeches, Arthur requested permission to make an announcement. He wished us to know, he said, he had been aware over the last few days of a furtive scrutiny directed by each of us toward the lower portion of his countenance. He would now inform us what we saw and mistrusted there was a budding beard. He considered this an appropriate occasion to have it recognized, identified and sanctioned. We expressed by resounding applause our gratitude for this enlightenment and relief to us. Howard betrayed that we had held secret conferences urging him to be the emissary to call Arthur's attention to an absent-mindedness that was permitting him to forget to complete his daily shaving. If this was not the reason for this curious outcropping, Dorothy would be happy to share her lotions had he become so sunburned as to make shaving painful.

I had the temerity to reveal one reason for our bewilderment at this phenomenon. Whatever it was it seemed to be gray, even white in places. For this reason we had flouted Howard's suggestion it might be a beard, pointing out Arthur's hair was black. Arthur admitted this incongruity had startled him. It had been one of the reasons he had not curtailed the burgeoning; he wanted to see how it would come out. Now that it had shown its true color he would like to entertain a vote either of confidence that it was becoming to him, or a veto. Sophy declared the floor open for discussion. It was recorded that Arthur must realize this made him look like Ernest Hemingway and must decide whether or not such a resemblance pleased him. Permitted to retain it he must maintain it with proper shaping and clipping, now that it was no longer a downy fledgling. Arthur having accepted this stipulation a vote was taken and passed unanimously that he be permitted and encouraged to be bearded at least until his daughter should see him; the final verdict should be left to her.

Arthur won again that afternoon at gin. Later that afternoon we came closer to an accident than at any other time during the whole cruise and Arthur was its near victim. When they had left the gaming table Howard had joined Dorothy, Sophy and me on the roof forward, but Arthur had gone on the one aft to doze in the sun, preferring exile to reproaches for winning. None of us saw him there. Howard said later he thought Arthur had stayed in the cabin. Mr. Walley and Mr. Fitter protested, in the later rehashing, they were under the same impression. We were at the mouth of a low bridge when Mr. Fitter, looking back to see if the stern was clear, caught sight of Arthur face down and far on one side of the roof. This was the one time when the boat had not been held to dead center. The pilots shouted simultaneously and Arthur by a miracle sensed he was in danger. Had he either stayed where he was or sat up to see what had happened he would have been badly injured. Instead he remained flat, but slithered toward the center and came through with only a scraped hand and sleeve. He had been sound asleep he said and was wakened by the shout. Something in its urgency startled him into full wakefulness immediately and realization, though he was face-down, of what the danger was.

Mr. Walley and Mr. Fitter were so shaken by this mishap Arthur spent a long time in conversation with them.

Mr. Walley conveyed to us the realization that had there been a real injury from such a cause he would have been professionally disqualified and disgraced. Furthermore in a shy, inarticulate manner standing on the ledge looking up at Howard, Dorothy, Sophy and me on the forward roof he let us realize Arthur was his hero. We had known they had long talks together, the two pilots and Arthur. Arthur had reported to us he had been surprised to find Mr. Fitter was a staunch conservative, but Mr. Walley was all for nationalization. We had heard Mr. Walley and Mr. Fitter after a chat with Arthur repeating to each other, with chuckles and an occasional guffaw, words and phrases he had used. We all did that however, savoring equally the rich flavor of his wit.

Mr. Walley did not know that day after day his idol and the Lindsays endeavored to match the Walley accent. Sometimes on the boat, frequently ashore, and certainly more than once a day they said aloud words from Mr. Walley's vocabulary and sentences in his manner, chiding themselves and one another at their inability to reproduce the cadence in which his words made hills and dales of each phrase. Sharpness of ear and an ability to reproduce accents are as primary requisites to an actor as a sense of color to a painter. I have heard Dorothy and Howard portray a Southerner or a New Englander with a veracity that could label them inhabitants of either of those locales. Yet they were never able to transplant Mr. Walley's Midlands cadence though they captured his pronunciation of words separately. It was a defeat they acknowledged, but to the end of our trip they continued to practice.

Over and over again I would hear them say such phrases

as "Aye, I will go oop ahn then I will coom doon" and each time break off with a "That's not it. I've got the words but not the rhythm."

We had seen Mr. Walley hover like an English Nanny over Arthur at the tiller, Arthur proud, but apprehensive —not more apprehensive than the rest of us that he should be at the wheel—Mr. Walley praising and encouraging him. But until Mr. Walley looking up at us from the ledge endeavored to let us know his actual grief at this mishap we had not understood that for him Arthur was not just a member of a cruising party, but a creature of spellbinding delight from a wonderful and witty but friendly world a bargeman had never known.

CHAPTER SIXTEEN

A LITTLE after five we went through the Heyford Mill lock and tied up there for the night. We went by car to the Hopcroft's Holt Inn at Steeple Aston, north Oxford, in Oxfordshire. The friends we were expecting from London had got there before us. Mr. and Mrs. Woodham-Smith and their son Charles waved us in. Cecil Woodham-Smith and her husband had been friends of mine and then of Sophy from the time a few years previously when she had come to America on the publication of her magnificent book *The Reason Why*. But the rest of the crew had not met them.

It had been at a dinner party at their house during the week in London between cruises this excursion had been planned. No further messages had been exchanged but it was entirely in character that on the day set and a little before the hour appointed they should arrive at the place stipulated. Of course we permitted ourselves the traditional "Mr. Livingstone, I presume," and immediately after invaded the bar, where Howard gave a splendid performance as a Martini mixer and according to nightly custom astounded the official bartender. Dinner was delayed while

Sophy and I went in the visitors' car at their insistence to show them the *Maid Marysue*. Woodham-Smith *père* is an enthusiastic and a skillful photographer. He took a great many pictures of the boat because the family reiterated none of them had seen, much less traveled on, one like it. Neither Sophy nor I gave responsive cries of "You don't mean it" to this statement because neither of us was in the least surprised by it. Two years before when Sophy and I had impulsively chartered a boat and cruised for one week on the Thames * we had learned, on our return, "one" did not travel on the river in that manner. This flock followed a dictum, the Lord knows whose, that "one" could row, punt or paddle but certainly not go in anything operated by an engine. However, we had also discovered individuals of this "one" group were so happily piqued by our chronicle of the delights to be had from such unorthodoxy they were even so bold as to contemplate trying it for themselves. The Woodham-Smiths had not been held back by any such social dam as this; they simply had never heard of the existence of such boats nor the possibility of such travel. By the time we were back at the hotel they had mapped out a voyage for themselves as soon as Cecil should have produced the book on which she was working.

Dinner was very gay. A superfluous note in my diary reads that Sophy made a speech.

On the basis of one to five Arthur said, ranging from country inn to Claridge's, he would count the Hopcroft's Inn a 4T hotel. It was far and away the best on our trip. Though they had all been pleasant, this one had both charm and comfort. It was very old; the original house, we were

Water, Water Everywhere.

told, had been a favorite rendezvous for a famous highway-man whose name I have forgotten. The bedrooms were low-ceilinged, attractively furnished and had casement windows that opened on a charming garden. Claridge's or any other London hotel does not provide better food.

The hotel at which we stayed the next night in Oxford was far and away the worst we encountered on the trip. I shall not repeat its name. I do not wish to remember it. The proprietor and his wife were pleasant, intelligent people but their place of business was neither comfortable nor clean. Nevertheless we were in Oxford. We had arrived shortly after lunch. We had eaten as we ran because this section of the canal is too close to the city of Oxford to have the charm we had found in the more remote countryside. A little above Oxford we tied up at a dock by a coalyard. Mr. Walley was sure before we left next day we would encounter a commercial barge, with coal to be unloaded here. We left him looking forward to a meeting with canal friends, but when he offered to introduce them to Mr. Fitter, whoever they might be, Mr. Fitter assured him he would not be around. He was off to the town to eat at a restaurant and "take in a flick."

I do not know how many miles we walked that afternoon in the beautiful town; but a drizzling rain was the only reason we stopped. Because it was so pleasant to have tea at The Mitre, we lingered on for cocktails and then dinner.

It was not late when we came back to our lodgings, and across the street through the uncurtained window of a pub I saw young men playing darts. At every country inn along the way I had asked to be shown people playing darts. From English novels I had supposed there was not an inn nor pub in the whole of the country that did not have a dart board on the wall of its bar; but not a single one we had visited could accommodate my request. The first evidence I had seen of what I had assumed was a village sport was in the large town of Oxford.

Dorothy and Howard would not be cajoled; they went on to bed. Arthur, though I detected a tone of something less than enthusiasm in his assent, did squire Sophy and me. We had an ale and we watched experts, because a gentleman at a nearby table told us two of these players were acknowledged champions. I saw them throw the darts and tally the scores. Neither activity came even in the neighborhood of my comprehension. The players seemed not to like getting near the bull's-eye, and as far as I could gather the scorekeeper offered congratulations when he subtracted rather than added. I gathered enough boldness to ask him to explain something of the system and within ten seconds regretted with all my heart I had not remained a silent spectator.

In my opinion England ought to gather up her lads who are now playing darts in pubs and put them to work on projected missiles and other problems of outer space. In the first place they like to lodge their missiles in an outer periphery. They do not care to be earthbound in a bull's-eye center, and in the second place they are lightning calculators, running up in no time a maze of figures they both compute and understand. I realize my word is not to be taken as that of a qualified judge since I never progressed mathematically beyond papering a wall, or carpeting a floor. Therefore, only wishing to be helpful, I call Great

Britain's attention to her untapped natural resources of mathematicians.

In my guileless way I had thought by showing genuine interest I might be invited to step up and have a try. This was one of the silliest ideas I ever entertained and my average is high. I have it in mind to write a letter to authors of English mystery stories who tell how they pick up knowledge of character and clues by going of an evening to the local pub, engaging in conversation and presently being invited to join in a game of darts. Writers I think should endeavor to be accurate.

After an hour spent almost uninterruptedly in silent meditation Arthur asked wistfully if I thought I had seen enough. Sophy said if I wanted to stay longer she was willing; she'd been dozing for some time she said and did not anticipate much choice between the wooden chairs on which we were sitting and our beds across the way. She was right. The pallets on which we spent the night were first cousins except in shape to the seats we had quitted.

We came to the dock and the *Maid Marysue* next morning a little after ten. We had been up early in order to change the position of our aching muscles. At breakfast, touching the toast, Dorothy had said to me, "Made at sunset last night, just as your father said." After breakfast we had taken a last walk. We had gone through stone arches and come upon enclosed quadrangles surrounded by gray walls or ivy-covered, and carpeted with bright young grass, then out again and presently along a narrow mews and into a hidden garden. It was "Speech Week" we were told, though perhaps we were mistaken in our surmise this was the end of a term. Certainly Oxford was not in its sleeping chrysalis stage I have seen in midsummer. Wherever we moved, students were around us, all of them in a hurry, all of them wearing mortar board and a short gown, an academic robe I had not seen before. Families were there too. It seemed unlikely any members could have been left behind there were so many ages in each clump, moving in a solid unit and pointing to one another particular sights. Their presence was the reason we had been unable to have lodging at The Mitre where we had hoped to stay.

We returned to our base, gathered up our bags and while we waited for the taxi that had been summoned by telephone, Dorothy set down rules for the next cruise.

"The only flaw in this one," she declared, "is we've gone too fast." This gave us a pause of astonishment. Howard filled it presently by pointing out fifteen miles, sometimes less, had been our daily coverage. Dorothy brushed aside impatiently his statistics.

"That's not what I meant at all," she said. "The speed has been just right but we've had to move whether we wanted to or not because of reservations at inns. It was wonderful to have them and be so well taken care of, but next time let's sleep on the boat; then we can stay over if we want to and most of the time we do."

We were still discussing this when the taxi unloaded us at the coalyard, and Dorothy was talking. She broke off in the middle of a sentence to point excitedly.

"Look," she said, "it *is* a barge unloading. Mr. Walley said there might be."

Mr. Walley had been right not only in his prophecy of the arrival of a barge but of the possibility of our going on

board. The bargeman and his wife were old friends. One at a time we went into their living quarters. There was not room for more visitors though our hostess whom Mr. Walley called Lil pointed out three small children playing on the dock as permanent occupants. It was exactly as I had heard and read it described. On the walls were racks of souvenir plates of cities and towns visited on their canal routes. There were gleaming brass ornaments though our hostess was apologetic about them.

"The coal dust settles over everything," she said ruefully, "but as soon as we get under way again I'll be polishing them up."

We saw painted tin receptacles like the ones Dorothy had purchased; but these were very old so the colors were softer than on hers. We marveled at the neatness in this tiny space and the crisp curtains in the windows, the cleanliness of everything except the people themselves, and this was understandable since the whole family helped with the coal. I hope when they were under way again and Lil got around to polishing up, she included the children. Sophy took pictures of the family; even Lil's husband was persuaded reluctantly to join the group. He put down the empty carrier he was returning to the barge for another load and wiped his hands carefully on his trousers before taking a pose beside Lil and marshaling the children in front. He need not have bothered to wipe his hands; from his head to his feet except for eyes and teeth he was "coal" black. When Sophy promised to send copies of the pictures, Lil shook her head dubiously. "I've 'ad 'em took before," she told us, "pictures that is and they always tell me surely they'll send one but they never do."

228

Sophy reiterated her promise and I echoed my assurance she would keep it. Lil shrugged her shoulders. "That's as may be," she told us. Nevertheless she left us for a minute or two and returned with two envelopes. She held one out to Sophy. "This will give you my name and address." Sophy read it aloud and Lil reached for it. "No," she said, "then that's the wrong one. Here 'tis," and extended the other. She could not read. Sophy read aloud the second one and made a copy when Lil verified it.

CHAPTER SEVENTEEN

Our way along the canal gave us a behind-the-scene view of the town. We saw charming gardens of houses whose faces were severe. We had seen many of them on our walks. Always in the distance there were high slender spires, the signposts of Oxford.

One does not expect to see a section of a railroad taken apart in order to permit a small boat to continue its holiday excursion and I venture to say one would not often encounter such an undertaking. But as we sat on the *Maid Marysue* in something of a trance of wonder, a crew of workmen gathered on a railroad trestle just ahead of us and fell to a task of removing bolts, subsequently sections of track, in order to permit the trestle to swing and allow us to pass under. This maneuver required close to three-quarters of an hour of hard work. Perhaps no train was scheduled to pass at that time or possibly by warning signal trains were delayed by the passage of the *Maid Marysue*. I cannot believe the replacement of track took any less time than its demolition and I shudder to imagine the temper of commuters in America halted for one hour and a half in deference to a small boat.

Under the bridge, a little run ahead around a curve and we moved into the River Thames. The canals we had traveled were behind us. We would not follow a narrow way again.

For Sophy and me it was a sort of homecoming. We had not only cruised on the river before but had traveled this very stretch of it.* But to the others, our emergence was as great a shock as though they had dived into it. The difference was hard to explain we said to one another. For nearly two weeks we had been traveling through wide-spreading country. We had not been in mountain gorges with high walls on either side like blinders to a view, but we had grown accustomed to the narrowness of the channels themselves, the neighborliness of the banks and certainly only one path to follow. Here a boat could wander, could choose its way. To be given such liberty was almost frightening. Dorothy paid a tribute to the river for all of us. We could not have offered a more fitting symbol of obeisance to its majesty. As we moved round the bend from the humble canal, Dorothy was halfway through a quick change. With a cry of wonder at the vista before us, she leaned far to one side to see more widely, clasped her hands, and said, "Look."

We looked, and among the dramatic sights within our view was Dorothy's pink-shirred nylon sun top floating on the Thames.

Within a short distance from the mouth of the canal we came abreast of the first of the Oxford barges and we very nearly lost crew member Stickney herself at this sight. In any moment of surprise or excitement she bends far for-

*Water, Water Everywhere.

ward in order to come nearer the object of her pleasure no matter what its distance from her. Her forward bend would have taken her from the roof to the Thames had Arthur not restrained her with a respectful firmness in the rear.

The barges make a splash of color in themselves. Anchored in stately file one immediately behind another they comprise a giddy, charming fleet of twelve. Each one belongs to a College of the University and at the races or other festivities are used for grandstands and tea parties. At other times they provide locker space for the crews. The vessels are large, broad, and flamboyantly caparisoned in gaudy colors. Their high ornate prows are brightly painted in absurdly rococo decorations; curved balconies take the place of decks. We laughed spontaneously with pleasure at the sight of them and mourned when I said I had read these hundred-year-old floats will be abandoned for more efficient quarters.

In the whole preceding ten days aboard the *Maid Marysue* there had not been such bustle as during the hour or so after we left Oxford. Dorothy, Howard and Arthur were constantly on the move from bow to stern, port to starboard and back again, pointing out to one another beautiful houses set well back from the river and glorious gardens between. Sophy and I nodded smugly like two indulgent Nannies. At a moment when we found ourselves alone we said hastily and confidentially to each other that, seeing the river now, we were appalled at our foolhardiness in having traveled on it alone, green as we were. Sophy said undoubtedly that was why we had done it; had we known anything we would have known better. On the other hand, had we not been foolhardy, this trip would never have come about.

The others, returning to ask the identity of something they had spotted, overheard the last part of this conversation and joined it. Arthur had a topic for speculative discussion, he said, and would like to propose it. Ever since his beard had been identified and endorsed, Arthur had shown a tendency to philosophic discussion and, while it was going on, would finger the little tendrils on his chin in a contemplative fashion. Dorothy asked him to wait while she brought her lotions and sweater from the cabin. When she had returned, spread them around her and begun her setting-up and taking-off exercises—only a sweater now the sun top was gone—she urged him to give us his argument and he obliged. If we were advising a friend, he said, on the way to take a cruise of this sort would we say to go from canal to river or start on the Thames? Religion, art or politics could not have provoked a livelier discussion but if voters were to veer and shift as frequently as we changed opinions they would succeed only in canceling out a candidate. Was the river appreciated the more if it came as a dramatic climax? On the other hand, would the canals hold greater surprise and enchantment if their narrowness and remoteness were accentuated by traveling the Thames first? In the end I think we agreed we would do it again exactly as we had done, saving the Thames for the last. Howard made a good point in favor of this. When you are nearing the end of a trip he said you have a little the feeling of being headed for the stables and so wanting to move along. This was an appropriate tempo for the Thames where there was traffic, but to end on the canal by hurrying would be a shocking thing to do.

We came into Abingdon at lunchtime. On a sudden impulse I suggested we tie up and go into the town to eat. We moored the boat at the very dock where Sophy and I had spent a night on our first cruise but we were disappointed to find the vivacious young woman who rented its space for overnight guests was away from home. There were geese, however, waddling along the towpath on the other side, and we knew how vicious they were. With shocking pleasure Sophy and I had watched them pursue and nip two elderly women.

The crew walked from the river to the Queen's Hotel. It is not far, by our own estimate, and the curving way passes the church and the old almshouses called Christ's Hospital. We paused of course to explore them. I had remembered them vividly and that is indicative of their charm.

We ate well at the Queen even though we had arrived when lunch was very nearly over. When we came out into the square, a bustling place, we discovered it had begun to rain while we were in the hotel. However it was not hard enough to warrant a taxi. Perhaps that was an unwise decision because walking back Dorothy and I saw an antique shop. Sophy and the men were ahead of us when we spied it. We did give them a halloo, but not a very loud one in case there should be dissension about our purpose. Sophy said later when they turned round to include us in their talk she felt for all the world as if she were in a preposterous fairy story; to be walking along a narrow cobbled stone street, little houses crowding its edge on either side, and then to turn about and find just as in the fairy stories the earth had swallowed up two friends who a minute before had been at her heels. But as she stared, Howard said one word that was like an abracadabra to solve the mystery. "Antiques," he pronounced, "somewhere back there."

Sophy found us. The men she said had gone on to the boat and would wait for us. Howard had sent word he did not wish to intrude, especially with money. We bought some things we loved. I did not know until she gave it to me for Christmas that Dorothy had managed to purchase and secrete a sizable and utterly irresistible Staffordshire lion. But she did not buy the owl lamp she saw and to this day there is no mention of the whole cruise that does not bring from her a wistful sigh and the same refrain, "I must go back for that owl lamp."

Soon after we left Abdingdon Sophy and I pointed out to the others two groups of trees on a distant hilltop, each group a dense, compact and almost perfect circle. We had been waiting for them with the eagerness one feels at the expected arrival of a friend one has not seen in a long time. Each of us was childishly endeavoring to be the first to spot them but we said, "There they are," almost in the same breath. They are called Wittenham Clumps or "The Crowns." Sometimes it is said they were planted in the eighteenth century but there is no record of whose planting it was. I have also heard it told they are far older than that and might have been a place of worship in England's antiquity. Whatever their origin there is no doubt about their dramatic beauty. Although not a barren landscape, this countryside does not include trees. The Crowns stand alone on a hilltop. These two dark green masses, high above the meadows, form a landmark that is visible for miles in every direction. It was visible to us during all that long afternoon. As the river curved we would be out of sight for a little while but inevitably the Crowns came into our view again.

The rain had stopped soon after we took off, the sun was warm. There was a great deal of bird life on view too, and human activity. Families of moorhens, herons and many more swans than we had previously seen. Fiercer too. One might have thought those on the canals would have been more aggressive since an intrusion occurred so infrequently. Sophy and I had been challenged, Dorothy had been chased and Howard had once bolted ignominiously into the cabin though he had pretended to be looking for something. By comparison, however, the rural swans were placid. Their sophisticated cousins on the Thames are well aware of the dangers of city traffic and just as belligerently and just as ineffectually as Paris gendarmes they do their best to halt it. Howard took a position on the roof. He stood at full height, feet apart, arms folded, cap pulled well down over his eyes to shield him from the sun. He said he found this the best way in which to see everything. Some of us entertained a wonder, unexpressed of course, if perhaps he had estimated this stance put him above soaring range of a long-necked attacker.

When Mr. Walley called, "Coomin' to a loock," Howard left his eminence and joined Arthur amidship; both of them ready to take on their accustomed duties. As we approached its mouth, saw its size and the massive gates that controlled it, Arthur, awed, said in a low tone he'd as soon think of offering his assistance in the operation of Hoover Dam as volunteer to lend a hand here. He broke off to point with a trembling finger toward the stern. "There's another boat coming in," he said shakily. "My God, doesn't the fool know any better? He'll crash us."

Sophy soothed him. "In these locks," she told him, "they pile up craft like automobiles on a ferry; they won't operate the gates until they've stacked in a full number when there are many waiting. If there are no others in sight they'll let us go on through."

We all went ashore to watch the operation by the lockkeeper and to admire his garden. Part of the duty of each keeper along the Thames is to maintain the garden that with the house is provided for him. There is a prize each year for the best of these. As a result they are during the summer immaculately kept, filled with bloom, and are among the prettiest sights on the river. Frequently the lockkeeper's wife has a little stand from which she sells bags of lavender and sometimes sweets and ice cream.

Either the monarchical position Howard had recently taken gave delusions of navigating grandeur or perhaps the operation of the locks by mechanism created the illusion the Thames was easy to handle. Whatever prompted such an idea I do not know, but I can assert we were put into a tremor of apprehension when banker Lindsay announced blandly he would like to take a turn at the wheel. Mr. Walley made no objection and for the first and only time on the cruise I considered the splendid man careless of the lives in his keeping.

Arthur, Sophy, Dorothy and I went as far off and as rapidly as possible. We huddled together at the very rim of the bow and there our doubts were substantially confirmed. Dorothy told us the kind of automobile driver her dear husband was. "He gives a wonderful performance," she explained, "of a skilled, almost professional driver in the way he sits, the way he holds the wheel. Everything about it is fine except the driving and that he does very poorly." Shortly after this analysis we saw a boat coming toward us. We said to one another what an unfamiliar sight this was after all our days on the canals when we had scarcely encountered any. A minute or two later Sophy observed, "Do you think Howard knows that in river traffic you pass on the right?"

"Surely Mr. Walley will tell him," was Arthur's answer but the assertion was not made positively.

A minute later Sophy spoke again. "Do you think Howard knows there is a boat coming toward us?" No one answered. It was Sophy who spoke again. "I can't stand it," she said, "I've got to tell him or find out, or do something myself." She half rose and turned back toward our helmsman. "Howard," she called coaxingly, "there's a boat coming toward us quite close."

We all turned to see how Howard would respond. He nodded toward Sophy indulgently, lifted a hand from the tiller in a sort of salute to all of us and answered, "He sees me."

I do not know how we passed each other; my eyes were closed, but I heard a request we watch what we were doing, made so close the owner of that voice might have been on our own deck. When I looked at the world again Mr. Walley was once more at the tiller. Howard was standing beside him feet wide apart, hands in his pockets, happy smile on his face. "Well," he said, "that was enjoyable. I'm sorry I didn't take over earlier on the trip. I must do more of it next time."

238

"You do that," Sophy muttered in my ear, "and I'll make a walking trip of the cruise, on the towpath."

vasiliu

I think the reason Mr. Walley invited Arthur to take us through a lock was his concern lest his hero might think favoritism had been shown Howard. The invitation was an unpleasant surprise to Dorothy and me. Howard favored it with the tolerant benignity of one who has won his spurs, though he had only steered the boat in the open river; he had not yet touched the gear shift. Arthur was at first demonstratively resistant. He flung his hands out toward the tiller as if to ward off its coming to grips with him, and backed away into the cabin. Nevertheless, perhaps because he did not want to disappoint Mr. Walley's estimate of his capabilities, he edged out again within a minute or two and asked our captain ingenuously, "Do you think I could do it?"

When I heard him say that, I knew we were sunk, or certainly in danger of sinking, because there was nothing in the whole world Mr. Walley would have thought impossible of Mr. Kober's accomplishment.

I did not have to hear his reassurance but Arthur listened to it with growing self-confidence as anyone could see from the way his shoulders went back and his spine stiffened into an admiral's rigor.

Mr. Walley gave him a few pointers about going in the lock but spoke apologetically as though these were only reminders of details that might have slipped Arthur's mind in his preoccupation with larger matters. When he had finished we could see the lock ahead. I looked at Sophy and saw she was pale. To give myself a little hope I said to her, "Well, after all, *you* did it."

"My God," was her answer, "at least I've sailed boats all my life. Arthur's never even rowed one. He's strictly an urban product."

Dorothy heard us, "Well maybe he has rowed," she quavered, "in Central Park."

She did not know, as Sophy and I knew, the hazards of locks in the Thames. It was all very well to run a boat in the narrow canal where the worst you could do would be to run into a soft bank. But to maneuver a lock involved avoiding other boats that might be coming out, holding back if we came up before the gates were opened and, once in, steering a course that would neither crash us into the stone wall nor across the way of another craft. And if all these hazards were avoided, we must be got out without ramming the gates before they were opened. He must not slew us sideways by not reckoning the force of the water coming in rapidly and filling that wide space. There were other perils but these were enough to think of at the moment, and they all raced through my mind.

"Where do you think we'd better go?" Dorothy asked in a small voice.

"Outside," Sophy answered decisively, "so we can jump."

We were at the door of the cabin when Arthur stopped us. Howard had joined in neither the conversation nor the exodus. He was stretched along the couch blandly reading a book. Arthur called his attention.

"I have something I wish to make known," he said, "before I execute this undertaking." Howard looked up. "Yes?" he asked.

"It is this," Arthur pronounced. "As temporary master of the ship I wish it clearly understood that in the event of foundering, the 'captain'" and he pointed to himself, "carrying the flag, is the first to leave the ship." He turned smartly on his heel and advanced to the tiller.

Howard took up his book again. Dorothy, Sophy and I left the cabin hurriedly and were immediately in a small panic. We did not wish to crowd Arthur by staying in the small area where the boat was run nor make him nervous by our evident agitation. On the other hand we could not

241

decide whether fore or aft would be the safer place. Sophy decided it.

"It won't make the slightest difference," she said. We went forward against my own inclination. In my cowardly fashion I would have preferred to be aft in order not to see what was about to happen, but let it come as a dreaded surprise.

Arthur led the *Maid Marysue* in and out of the lock as if he were a master mariner, descendant of a long line of seafaring folk.

When we were in the open water again he made no

verbal answer to our babbling congratulations, Mr. Walley's and Mr. Fitter's resounding slaps on his back, nor Howard's incongruous comment, "Handles nicely, doesn't she?" He went without words into the aft cabin where he and Howard kept their changes of costume. When he reappeared a minute or two later, he was wearing a yachting captain's cap a friend had given him in New York as a bon-voyage joke. Arthur had shown it to us with amused embarrassment. "Could you imagine my wearing such a thing?" he had asked.

From that time on I never saw him on the boat without that cap on his head and at a rakish slant. We called him "captain" and he referred to us as "my crew."

As we were leaving the boat that night Howard said, startled, "Arthur, do you realize we didn't get in our gin today?"

"I know," Arthur told him. "I was busy."

CHAPTER EIGHTEEN

WHEN Sophy and I had spent a night at Pangbourne on our Thames cruise we had tied up at precisely the spot where the *Maid Marysue* moored. The landmark was a house that when Sophy and I first saw it was the very model of a haunted ruin. The lawn had been ankle high in weeds, the front steps rotted almost away, the windows without glass, most of them, some with jagged remnants of panes. The very style of the house with foolish cupolas and fretwork was an invitation to haunting. It had been purchased since our visit and was now in the process of a renovation to suburban respectability. Sophy and I were disappointed and so was Dorothy because we had guaranteed to scare her.

The weir had not changed. Kenneth Grahame had lived in Pangbourne and this weir is the residential district of Mr. Mole and Toad of Toad Hall in *The Wind in the Willows*. The road from the river to the town passes it. The five of us paused for a long time to look, in the soft light that in an English summer is not yet twilight, at the willows bending down to touch the water, the little flying insects that come out in the late afternoon and prickle its surface, and the erratically sudden shiver of reeds at the edge where per-haps Mr. Mole was passing by.

Dinner at the George Hotel was good and its beds were comfortable but I did not go to sleep for a long time. This was the only night such a thing had happened to me on the cruise. Arthur had not slept at Southam as he had reminded us more than once, but except for that one night, we were all so heavy-eyed with delicious sleepiness after a day slowly passed in the warm sun, we had gone each night to bed and to sleep at a school child's hour.

I was wakeful in Pangbourne and also for the first time I was impatient to move on. The reason was a note at the hotel, waiting our arrival. It was the memorandum of a telephone message received from the vicarage in Cookham.

One of our friends from the Inland Waterways had evi-dently heard me talk about the bell ringers there and must have telephoned we were coming. The message read, "The bells can be rung any time from seven to eight o'clock but not from eight to nine because there is a service. The vicar would be happy to arrange for the bells to be rung as the boat approaches Cookham if he can be let know the approximate time of arrival."

This was the bell ringing I had described to Arthur when I had asked him to come on the trip. It is described too, in *The Nine Tailors,* Dorothy Sayers' book I had pressed on him to read and he had not enjoyed. Neverthe-less he had admitted he would like to hear the ringing itself. Sophy and I had heard it by accident on that other trip. One day more and then we would hear it again and the others to whom I had talked, tediously I know, would experience it for the first time, and not forget it. Of that

I was sure. Only one day's run to go, starting as early as we always started, we could be there, Sophy had told me from the map, by midafternoon. That would let us explore the town, visit the beautiful church itself before the bell practice, though we would hear them from the water, thanks to their hospitable offer. Kings and queens and admirals, I thought, as I moved restlessly on my bed, are piped aboard a ship, but we are going to be rung ashore—the most dazzling red carpet ever spread before arriving guests.

We were not rung ashore and we were not in Cookham by midafternoon. We did not even reach Cookham by water; we came in a taxi from Marlow where we had gone aground.

We were as good as aground at Pangbourne for four hours because the engine broke down. On any other day of the cruise or in any other spot I would not in the least have minded the engine's stopping for almost any length of time, but that it should happen on the only day I wanted so urgently to get on was an exasperation that roused in me a fervor to kick the silly cogs and wheels.

We had no news of this misfortune until we reached the dock at nine o'clock on the morning after my wakeful night. Mr. Walley had learned it only a short time before when he had prepared to run a brief distance ahead to a nearby gasoline pump. He and Mr. Fitter had begun working on the engine at once and only a few moments before we came had realized they would have to telephone for help and put in a call. Someone was coming with the part that had to be replaced but this would take some time. Our cruises have been lucky but on each of the few times something untoward has occurred, it has inevitably been at a spot that could not have been pinpointed with more accuracy as most remote from assistance. In all honesty I admit, had we been on a stretch of canal, assistance would have been inaccessible. But on that morning in Pangbourne learning we could not get away for at least three hours I had no mind to believe things could have been worse.

Hearing the news, Arthur and Howard promptly went back to visit the town, since we had arrived too late for exploring on the evening before. I proposed to accompany them but stop off for marketing. I reminded them bitterly we had thought to reach Cookham in time for a late lunch and the plan had included an extra-early start since we would not have to take time for buying provisions. I declined assistance from Dorothy and Sophy. I would not buy enough to warrant it, I told them, and said to myself I was too disgruntled for companionship or conversation. Dorothy would go to the roof, she said, as soon as she had changed. She ought to be able to get in an uninterrupted exposure for tanning, since she explained carefully we would be standing still; therefore she would not have to make adaptations of costume to an errant breeze.

Each of these programs seemed to all of us sensible and in one way or another useful, but Sophy's, when she divulged it, seemed to the rest of us preposterous and incredible. She planned, she said, to walk along the path to a place nearby where she had seen boats advertised for hire. She would engage one and go for a row. When one of us ventured to ask why, she answered, in some surprise, it would seem to her obvious: she wanted exercise. She had it. For two hours she rowed up and down the river across to its far bank and back, around several times in a wide circle.

247

I doubt any busman could match his sort of holiday with hers. I sometimes think of a couple who passed her during her outing and wonder what conclusion they drew from their brief exchange of words. I heard the man call out to her, "Lovely day. Going downriver?"

"Yes, isn't it? No, I'm just waiting for a boat."

Immediately after that bright repartee I went shopping. I will remember that day for a number of "firsts" that happened: the engines breaking down, Sophy's curious excursion and my departure for the market with a string bag in either hand. It is an admission of idiocy to report that not once had the one who was doing the shopping remembered the equipment, nor any of the stay-behinds thought to remind her. Of all the crew Howard was far and away the most consistently mindful of things to be taken ashore and brought back. He never forgot anything except those wretched string bags. He would say as we left the boat each night, "Emily, have you your camera? Be sure to bring your topcoat, it may be chilly when we walk after dinner. Sophy, you have your maps, haven't you? We'll want to look for anything in the vicinity we might want to see," and so on through the separate requirements of each of us. In spite of protest from us he carried the greater part of Sophy's and mine as well as Dorothy's. Arthur always offered but could be dissuaded. Howard was adamant. He accoutered himself like a pack mule, his original shape scarcely discernible from boat to car, car to inn, and yet not once did he think of string bags. When we chided him about this, only because he was the one who always remembered everything, he expostulated marketing was not within his line of duty. The retort to that from the women

248

was that, considering the groans and reproaches from him each time one of us had to tell him to mark down in his bankbook the price of two string bags, we would have thought reminding us less painful to him.

Shortly after noon the engine was working again and we were on our way. Had we left in the early morning perhaps the rowing crews would not have been in practice on the course at Henley. When I pointed this out, Sophy commented I was showing signs of regaining my temper. I would certainly during the morning hours not have been of a mind to offer any compensation for our delay.

The shells came toward us as we approached and we caught almost as much excitement as the race itself would have brought because of the beauty of rhythm, the oars flashing in the sun, dipping quickly to a long even sweep. The course itself runs down the center of the stream and is set apart by a floating barricade, on either side, of logs lashed one to another. This is hallowed water, of course; other traffic proceeds along the side channels.

The races were to take place the following week, and seeing this rehearsal, the Lindsays and Arthur promised one another they must come without fail. Sophy and I would be gone; she flying to Africa and I going to Paris for a last visit with my family. We had seen the races another time and reiterated it was a sight that should not be missed. There were few to be found more colorful and gay. However on the days of the races we admitted they would not have such an uninterrupted view as ours of this practice. Then these side passages would be choked with craft of every sort. There would be no moving of position, as we were moving. If you were on a boat you would be lucky to find a spot in which to stop, and if you did, your stop would be maintained by necessity until the last race was finished. The shore would be crowded with people in covered grandstands and on rows of chairs in the open; other crowds without seats walking about or moving as much as they could through the crush. Facing them on the opposite bank would be members of a more stylish audience belonging to the club that would have tables set out on a cov-

ered balcony and other special places for privileged guests. The members of the diplomatic corps who came would be seated there. The very contrast between the two sides of the river would make the whole pageantry even more colorful.

The stamina of the British is something astounding. Sophy pointed out a verification of this the rest of us had not noticed because we were concentrating on the shells. A coach on the path across from us was shouting his instructions through a megaphone that he held in one hand. The other hand grasped the handlebar of a bicycle. He was riding at the pace the crew of the shell was maintaining and shouting besides. I have seen other coaches and other crews but I had never seen a coach pedaling a bicycle at racing speed and shouting in full voice at the same time.

Someone from the bank shouted at us as we were nearing Marlow but none of us understood what he said until the *Maid Marysue* indicated by jarring us a little that we were aground. Mr. Walley had been on the Thames only once before in his years on a barge, he told us. Though Mr. Fitter had been asked to share the responsibility for the very reason that he knew the river though not the canals, he had not known, excusably, that this small unmarked stretch not far from the dock must not be covered on a short cut; it was necessary to come abreast of the landing and then turn in.

After considerable maneuvering we poled ourselves afloat again but by this time it was too late to continue by water if we were to hear the bells. The area along the bank in this section is a sort of public park. People were enjoying the late afternoon there and most of them I should think gathered on the bank where we were unwillingly attached. With characteristic British reticence they watched us in silence. In America the clamor of advice would have been deafening. Sophy animated the group by calling into it an earnest request for one of its members to telephone for a taxi if there was a call box handy. There was and several young men murmured embarrassedly they would be glad to oblige.

When we stepped onto the dock one of these couriers told us a taxi was waiting at the entrance to the park. We drove to Cookham through a countryside that surprised us. Almost immediately we had left the river we were in decidedly hilly country. The road was not mountainous but it was steep with many curves and vistas opening out as we rounded them, stretches of woodland between. It was a lovely drive for which I had little appreciation. By this time I was superstitious as well as impatient. There seemed to be something implacable in the obstacles that had been thrown across our way to prevent my doing the only specific thing on the entire cruise that demanded our reaching a particular place at an appointed time. Two setbacks in one day and on the only day that mattered made a provocation, by the rule of superstition, to anticipate a third.

It did not come. Whatever may have been threatening veered off.

We arrived at the White Hart Hotel, dropped our bags and ran down the street to the Bell and Dragon, that I count one of the best restaurants in England. We had a succulent and leisurely dinner, excellently served. We were unhurried now we had reached our destination because the eight-o'clock service was taking place. We would hear and see the bells rung after nine. As we were leaving I asked Arthur how he would rate this establishment. He smiled dreamily the lazy smile of a contented and well-filled inner man.

"Throw in the towels," he said. "This place is too good for counting."

Mrs. Ethridge was waiting for us at the entrance to the churchyard. She was one of the bell ringers and had been cordial and hospitable to Sophy and me that other time when we had trespassed on their practice. She introduced us to the vicar, who had come with her to greet us, a charming vigorous young man. At the moment of our arrival he was giving advice to a parishioner who was endeavoring to back his car out of a very small space. The advice was as skillful a blending of the practical with the spiritual as I have heard.

He stood in front of what in England they call the bonnet of the car facing the driver and pantomiming with both hands, his clerical robe caught up like a bride's train over his arm.

"A little to the left," he called. "That's right, hold it. Pull to the left." Then he ran to the open window by the driver, put his head in and exhorted earnestly, "Have faith, man, have faith." He left the window, returned to his former position and resumed his specific instructions. He maintained this balance of advice until the car was in the clear and on its way. That completed, he came over to where we stood and greeted us cordially.

Bell ringing in England is a very old art. Most of the people who practice it are descendants of a long line of bell ringers and begin their training early. They are such enthusiasts, Mrs. Ethridge had told Sophy and me, their happiest pattern for a holiday is to visit other churches where bells are rung and be allowed to substitute for one of the regulars. Returning home from such a trip they do not recite to their friends the places they have seen, but tell instead the bells they have rung.

The bells themselves are not rung in the tower in which they hang. Dorothy Sayers in *The Nine Tailors* makes a plot of a catastrophe that can occur from too close proximity to such reverberation. Ropes hang from their clappers to a room on the floor below. This is where the ringers work. Each rope is wound round in colors. The only ones I have seen were red, blue and white combined; perhaps these are the traditional colors, I do not know. The bells themselves vary in size and tone, of course. Each is named and numbered; the largest, number one, is the Granddaddy. If you were to ask the players to give you a tune they would be scandalized at such indignity to their profession. A tune they count as a mawkish thing fit for organs or for the chatter of carillons. A bell ringer does not play anything, he "rings changes." A change is the term for a sequence of variations on the juxtaposition of bells. Instead of music written by note these artists follow a chart of numbers. The changes themselves like musical compositions have names but these compositions look like pages from a book on higher mathematics. There is pride in the number of changes that have been rung on a special occasion. On one of the walls in the bell-ringing room in the Cookham tower there is a framed citation of the changes rung on a particular Sunday morning to welcome the vicar we had met, when he had come to this parish the preceding year.

When I read this citation I did not mark down the number. I am confident I am guessing far too low when I say over two thousand. I think the actual number was over five thousand. I remember distinctly the performance lasted over five hours without a break. If once during that time a single ringer had lost count the whole ceremony would have had to stop. There is no picking up again as there is in other music. Each ringer is dependent on the preceding tone for his own count and the counts go something like one over two, two under three, meaning that on a particular round each bell waits one or two or three or whatever according to the pattern. The ringing itself, Mrs. Ethridge explained, is not difficult, though, she added thoughtfully, it was easy enough to break an arm if one hadn't the trick of it. When the bells are not in use they are turned clapper up. The first thing that must be done at practice or performance is to swing them down. It takes a strong man to do this and a skillful one. He must know just when to pull and when to release in order not to be himself jerked into the air and possibly suffer a broken bone. The actual pulling is not difficult but it requires acute sensitiveness in order not to allow the bell to develop such motion it will swing all the way round and up again, taking the ringer with it. Therefore he must count, feel and watch all at the same time. For this reason too there can be no exchange of conversation. At a long session, Mrs. Ethridge said, they sometimes suck lozenges because the throat can become very dry. She said nothing about the condition of the arm muscles and only smiled when Arthur reminded her of this. "It's just a matter of getting used to it," she told him.

She was explaining this as we walked across the churchyard and she made no pause while we climbed the perilously steep winding stone steps up and up into the tower. The sounds of heavy breathing filled this little enclosure but they came from the rest of us. She continued to speak evenly and effortlessly. When we were at the top and in their quarters she showed us the citations on the walls, and the manuscripts of some of the changes, those pages of mathematics. She introduced us to the other ringers, all this without so much as a single catch of breath. We stood against the wall while the ringers took their places in a circle, each with a hand on a bell rope. Mrs. Ethridge with a nod of her head gave the cue and they were off. From overhead as the ropes went up and down came a wild, strange weaving of sound. The only recognizable thing was the identification by its timbre that the instruments were bells. The sounds themselves overlapped so there was not even a decisive rhythm to hear, though watching you could count a steady beat. There was change of neither tempo nor volume, no shading from pianissimo to fortissimo, and yet there was emphasis by the very tones themselves and the dying away of successive sounds, then their reappearance. This made for a range of modulation from loud to soft but it was not obvious. Though there was no tune to remember the very wildness and strength and exciting clamor I still carry in my head.

We were taken up another flight of stairs to see the great bells themselves, but only after the music, if that is what it was, had stopped and the bells had been upended again. They were magnificent things in a dark bare room. We said to one another we could well believe shut up in the small enclosure, and the giant clappers sounding, madness, deafness or death would be inevitable.

When we came downstairs again into the churchyard we

urged Mrs. Ethridge and the other ringers to come with us back to the Bell and Dragon where we might talk, but they were either shy or genuinely in a hurry to be at home. We had kept them late. They overrode our gratitude with emphatic insistence that they appreciated so much our coming and our interest.

The vicar had left us at the beginning of the ringing and we did not find him when we left the church, but some time after we had reached the Bell and Dragon and were having beer and talk he came in with a visiting clergyman. They had gone first to the inn where we were stopping in the hope of finding us, but when we were not there had turned confidently to this place.

Because I had a somewhat puritanical bringing-up I was abashed at being tracked to a pub unerringly by two men of the cloth and found there with a tankard of beer. I thought it would be affected however to make some sort of apology and that the best thing would be to pretend it wasn't there at all. I therefore flung myself into conversation, ignoring my tankard. After a few moments I realized both the clergymen were regarding mine and the others' rather pointedly and yet it seemed to me there was something other than censure in their manner. I took a deep breath and plunged. If my friends and I were giving them provocation to hurl us into the fires of hell because we had been found tossing off beer and ale, I might as well hear the imprecation aloud and so I gave them opportunity.

In a faint voice I asked, "Would you by any chance care for a little glass of beer?" I made it small in order to keep the coming damnation to size as well. The two men of the church shook their heads simultaneously and wistfully. It was the visitor who spoke. "It's after closing hours now," he said reproachfully. "Pity."

Dorothy and I found antique shops the next morning but I was dissuaded from taking away two chairs in the hand and the owner was baffled by the complications of shipping them. I will go back for them when Dorothy returns to Abingdon to purchase her owl lamp.

We picked up the boat again just below Cookham where the captain had brought it the day before. The day was beautiful, the sun warm and every prospect delighted the eye, one lovely garden after another since we were no longer in remote untended country. As Dorothy pointed out with a slight shudder, any of this formal planting could have provided such a flower arrangement as the one at Aynhoe Park. Somehow our spirits were not high. We pointed sights to one another but instead of the shrill excitement of the first sweep of the river, there was an atmosphere over us of gentle melancholy, the sort that had heretofore only been Howard's at the immediate close of a gin game.

We diagnosed our complaint that evening as we were having drinks in the delightful garden of the White Hart Hotel in Windsor. What ailed us we agreed was we were coming to the end of the cruise and we did not want it to end. We were not looking forward to London for all the entertainment and diversion it would offer. We understood clearly why barge people kept to the water and looked with distrust and some disdain on human beings running about the land. The barge people showed good sense, we agreed.

We walked about Windsor Castle and were impressed. In the evening after dinner we walked across the bridge and were in Eton. We strolled among its buildings and admitted their charm and their dignity, but our hearts were not in our sightseeing. We were more aware of tired feet than of edifying sights.

The next morning we were in happier temper although this was our last day. I think we had become resigned to inevitability and determined to make the most of what remained. Howard was conspicuously off our lighter key. He was silent and withdrawn. He acknowledged the lovely things we pointed out, and our efforts to brighten him, with remote courtesy. When we stopped at Hampton Court and learned we were too late for lunch, the dining room was closed, Howard was no more depressed than he had seemed during the morning. Ices were the only thing the neighborhood offered. We stood in a little sweet shop eating these as rapidly as possible yet not fast enough to prevent leakage through the paper containers to our hands, but Howard was indifferent to this annoying discomfort.

It was when we were leaving the shop wiping disgustedly our sticky fingers that he unburdened himself of his sorrow. It came in answer to the suggestion from Sophy we pay our respects to Hampton Court.

"Yes," he said, with a vehemence that startled us, "I will go to Hampton Court and I will endeavor to lose myself in the maze there so that Dorothy will go on to London without me."

Dorothy's eyes widened at this. She said it was the first and only indication she had ever had of the possibility of a rift. The others of us were more shocked at his choice of locale. "Why, Howard," I said, "you mean you want to leave the water? Then why for heaven's sake are you so depressed?"

That gentle man squared away. "Because," he said, "I am faced with the prospect of marching into the Savoy Hotel strung all over with painted tinware. I've spent two weeks changing my clothes in a cabin in order to present an inconspicuous appearance at a country inn with only a handful of people at best to see me. I will now walk through the crowded lobby of a London hotel looking like something between an old junk peddler and a circus wagon."

By the time we had completed the tour of Hampton Court we had arrived at a solution. The Lindsays would be the only passengers in a car that would take them back to London. Arthur, Sophy and I would engage another. The Lindsays' car would include Howard's vivid caparison. It would take them and their owners direct to the firm that had shipped other things for them, though this address was on the far side of London from the Savoy. Nevertheless at whatever hour they reached it they would walk into the Savoy as inconspicuously as they had entered any inn along our route.

We had no sooner extricated Howard from this maze when he put his head into another. At the moment of his re-entry he was walking through a gallery with the women. Arthur had dropped behind to examine a picture.

"I'm a little troubled," Howard confided, "about our extra disbursement to Mr. Walley. It will be my last official duty and I want it to be correctly done."

261

We tested aloud various sums and settled on three pounds. Sophy clarified the amount. "It's a little under ten dollars."

Howard nodded pontifically. "Just right, I'd say. I'll tell Arthur what you suggest and see what he thinks."

Two minutes later, possibly less, the hall reverberated with a man's voice raised in amazed dismay. We made out words.

"Good God," echoed through that vast chamber. "I knew the girls were devoted to Walley, but this is hero worship. TEN POUNDS?"

We hurried back to the men. We soothed Arthur, reminded Howard three pounds had been set as a little under ten DOLLARS.

Arthur was mollified, Howard optimistic.

"I think I've got the hang of British currency now," he assured us. "Next time I'll have no anxieties."

Two cars were waiting for us at Thames Dytton because we had telephoned from Hampton Court. We stowed our respective belongings in each of them. We said good-by to Mr. Fitter and Mr. Walley. Mr. Walley lingered a little over his farewell to Arthur. Mr. Fitter would go back to the job from which he had taken a holiday in order to help us. Mr. Walley would return to his maintenance crew on the canals, but before he did that he would spend the night in London. This would make the second sight of that city in his life, he told us. He said too he would have much to tell his Missus when he got home, not only about London but about the cruise with us.

I wonder how he has described us. I think of him on

a winter evening in his little house on the canal bank at Newport repeating to the Missus in his own accent the things Arthur had said.

Between the dock and the waiting cars Dorothy stopped. She turned and went back to the boat. We thought she

had forgotten something and we waited. She walked to the bow of the *Maid Marysue*, leaned over and patted it with a maternal briskness.

"Next time, dear," she said, "we won't leave you at night."

GLOSSARY

from *Cruising on Canals* *

Water cans   The lids blow off if they are not tied on.

Pillow covers   The stiff covers are for use as cushions and can be removed at night.

Pound   A stretch of canal between locks. It may be 100 yards or 10 miles long.

To drop a paddle   To close or wind down a paddle.

To draw a paddle   To open, to wind up.

Narrow lock   A lock 7 feet wide.

Broad lock   14 feet wide.

Strap   A boat's mooring rope.

Lock wheeler   A person who goes ahead to prepare locks when close together.

Sill   The stone or iron ledge projecting into the lock below the top gate. *Beware of letting your stern catch on it when descending.*

Paddle post   The post at the side of a lock (usually at the top end) from which the ground paddles are wound up and down.

Paddle   The invisible sliding panel in the gate of a lock or in an underground sluice that, when open, lets water

* Distributed by Canal Cruising Company, Ltd., Stone, Staffs., England (Copyright).

264

pass from the top pound into a lock or from the lock into the lower pound.

Pawl The iron catch which prevents the paddle from falling when up. It must click on the cog wheels when you are winding up. Only lift it to wind the paddle down. It is not found on every canal.

Windlasses Are supplied for each journey, Trent & Mersey (red), Grand Union (green), all other canals (blue). See that you have those you require. They cost 15/- each to replace. They are frequently left behind or dropped in the canal. *Never* lay them on the balance beam when opening gates.

Passing moored boats *Always* slow down or you may cause them to break their mooring straps. Other boats will do this for you.

In locks When descending let the engine tick over in neutral. Ascending keep it in the forward gear and fast enough to hold the boat steady. The person left on the boat must know how to control the engine.

Passing boats Passing other pleasure boats keep to the right and not more than one foot apart. Passing a narrow boat keep out of his way and take whichever side seems best. On a corner take the inner side. *Slow down before you pass.* He cannot afford to run aground and his boat weighs 35 tons loaded.

Bridge holes These vary in height. Do not assume that your boat will not touch until you are sure. Beware of a gust of wind as you go through. Keep near the towpath side but do not cannon off it. If you cannot see ahead sound your horn. It requires skill to shoot a bridge hole and not touch so it is better to slow down until you are skillful.

Winding   (Short *i*, as in "windy.") I.e., turning round. *Venturer* can only wind at junctions or winding holes. Other big boats will need a broad spot. Don't use the engine except on broad rivers. Turn the nose sharply in to the non-towpath bank at a wide spot. Take the stern strap on to the towpath and pull the stern round, *keeping the stern away from* the bank with the shaft.

HOW TO TAKE A BOAT
THROUGH A LOCK

This is quite a simple thing to do IF YOU KNOW HOW. But if you don't, you may do serious damage to the boat, or run the canal dry and pay for refilling it. We have compiled these instructions so that you may study them before you come on your holiday and also refer to them while cruising. If you find them difficult to understand, remember that we shall take you through two locks at the start of the cruise, giving you careful instruction and making you work the locks yourself.

The important things are:

1   To know the lock drill off by heart and in the right order.
2   To see that the paddles you shut are properly shut.
3   To see that the person left on the boat knows what to do in a lock.

NO. 1   is dealt with below.

NO. 2   (a) When you wind a paddle *down* give it a jerk to make sure it is right down.

(b) See that the paddle bar is right down, not sticking up.

(c) If water is still flowing through the paddle, open and shut it again, which may loosen some obstruction. But old paddles tend to leak.

(d) If you find gates and paddles at both ends shut, please leave them all shut.

NO. 3 When *descending* a lock keep the bows by the bottom gates. If she drifts her stern may catch on the SILL. This will smash your rudder if nothing worse.

When *ascending* a lock the bows must be touching the end wall, with the engine in forward gear, i.e., pressing against the end wall BEFORE anyone opens the ground paddles to fill the lock. Otherwise the boat will be out of control and be thrown about by the incoming water. If the engine stalls, drop all paddles. If there is broken brickwork in the side wall see that the gunwale does not catch on it. If the top gate leaks shut your bow doors.

Before you *fill* a lock with water from the top pound you must see that the bottom gates and paddles are shut. Before you *empty* a lock you must see that the top paddles (ground and gate) and the top gates are shut.

TO DESCEND A LOCK, e.g., going south from Stone.

(a) If the lock is EMPTY:

1   Bring the boat gently to shore near the top gate. Send your lockworkers ashore *with* their windlasses.

2   Shut the bottom gates and the paddles on these gates. Lift the pawls.

3   Draw (open, wind up) the ground paddles on the paddle posts, and the paddle on the top gate. (Don't lift the pawls.) This will fill the lock.

4   When the lock is full open the top gate and take your boat in. Put her nose to the bottom gates, gently. Remember the sill behind you.

5   Shut the top gate. Shut the ground and top gate paddles (properly).

6 Draw the paddles on the bottom gates which will empty the lock.

7 When the lock is empty, open the gates and take the boat out. (If the gates won't open it may mean that a top paddle is not properly shut.)

(b) If the lock is FULL proceed as from No. 4 above.

L'ENVOI

A letter from Mr. Walley to Sophy. He will forgive me for not correcting his few mistakes in spelling, nor adding to his punctuation. I would not for the world change the cadence they bring to the reading.

> 6 Water Lane
> Newport Salop.

Dear Mrs. Jacobs.

I thank you very much for the snapshots and your letter my family and I were very thrilled with the snaps and we allso got a copy of the Life magazine.

I have given the snaps you sent to the boat woman and she was very pleased with them I wanted to do this before writting to you.

The weather broke a few days after out trip and it as not been very good ever since I am glad Miss Kimbrough as got well again and the rest of the party are o.k.

> Yours Sincerely
> J. Walley

I count the following letter one of the most curious coincidences in timing I have experienced. I received it

270

three days after I had written the episode of Sophy's and my meeting with Miss Ritchie. We must have been writing simultaneously.

6th June 1958

DEAR MISS KIMBROUGH,

I wonder if you happen to remember me? I moored next to your boat at Aadlem Town Lock in the Shropshire Union Canal last summer, and we watched the narrow boat crews bow-hauling their way through the lower lock there? You then went on your way towards the Welsh Union canal and Madame Pandit? I enjoyed our brief meeting very much, and have always recalled it when I have passed by Aadlem since—a matter of five or six times, I suppose. I was however, *more* than vividly reminded of it at 2 A.M. this morning, and it amused me *so* much I am writing to tell you about it!

I am moored in "Curlew" by Market Drayton Bridge, as I go to Brittany on Monday on a bicycling tour. In the middle of last night I woke up to hear the unmistakeable sounds of a heavy boat which had broken loose. A large cruiser had moored above "Curlew" late in the evening, but I hadn't noticed much about her. I checked that it wasn't my own boat floating about—as the wind had risen and then looked out. The next boat was in obvious difficulties, so I went out to see if I could help. It turned out to be two Americans, rather new to boats and canals, but very enthusiastic about their holiday so far. We recaught the boat and moored her fast, and during this process, bellowing against wind and weather as you can imagine, they told me they were over here as a result of an account in

271

"Life" of a canal holiday by two of their fellow-country women. I said did it happen to be you mentioning your name—rather as you can imagine, on the lines of "Mr. Jones of London," but it *did* turn out to be you and your friends! I *was* so amused, and I am sure all one needs to do here is to tie up on the Shropshire Union and wait for Americans to navigate by. Anyway, we got their boat re-captured, re-moored, and an anchor I keep for emergencies firmly attached to them, and they appeared to have survived the night quite satisfactorily. Today I have shown them how to moor, and have contacted the Nanturch Boat Club so that the members now up the Welsh Union can keep an eye on them if they need anything; they seem quite enthusiastic about their holiday and have a good boat. A new firm has started at Fradley, and appears to have *really* good boats for hiring I am pleased to say—really well equipped. It is a good thing and was much needed.

The canals themselves are the same as you will remember them. I have been to Llangollen quite recently, and did so enjoy it. In August I take my boat north to Shipton to be nearer my home, and where I shall be working in a Hospital after September.

I hope very much that all goes well with you and yours; and that the new grandchild who was due to arrive in Paris, I believe, sometime last summer put in a good appearance and by now is flourishing exceedingly.*

With very best wishes,
Yours sincerely,
J. MURIEL RITCHIE
m/c "CURLEW"

*Note: Alis arrived on July 31st.

SUGGESTED READING

Stanford's Inland Cruising Map of the Canals and Rivers.
Know Your Waterways.
English Rivers and Canals, by Frank Eyre and Charles
 Hadfield. William Collins Sons & Co., Ltd., London.
Cruising on Llangollen Canal.
British Transport Waterways.
*Historic Houses and Castles in Great Britain and Northern
 Ireland.* Index Publisher Ltd., 69 Victoria St., London.
Narrow Boat, by L. T. C. Rolt. Eyre & Spottiswoode, Ltd.,
 London.
The Narrow Search, by Andrew Garve. Harper & Brothers,
 New York. A mystery novel that includes excellent de-
 scription of operating locks.

BASIC EXPENSES

Hire fee for *Venturer*	£29 per week
Charge for lad	£6 per week
Hire fee for *Maid Marysue*	£33 per week